A Plate of Grace

Recipes from
the Westerbeke Ranch Kitchen

Carol Cleveland Bojarsky

Hungry Heart Press • Sonoma • CA • 1991

A Plate of Grace
by Carol Cleveland Bojarsky

Published by Hungry Heart Press
2300 Grove St. Sonoma, CA 95476

Aysha Griffin, *Project Editor*
Wendy Westerbeke, *co-Publisher*
Karen Leen, *Marketing Support*

Illustrations and Cover Design by Donna Bailey

Book Design by Joel Wastell, Graphico, Sonoma, CA
Printing by Seraphim Rose Press, Forestville, CA

Back Cover Photograph by David Helling

Other Photographs from the Westerbeke Ranch Archives

 Printed on recycled paper

ISBN 0-9632142-0-9

As my life unfolds it seems it is becoming ever more real and ever more heavenly. The facts are often tedious; diapers, teething, working mother, endless dishes and laundry, sleepless nights on one side, demanding schedules, menus, flies, broken dishwashers on the other. But the spirit is in ecstasy, flowing joyfully over the plate of this life that's been dished out to me. Along with the recipes that's what I want to share—that cooking and serving the fruits of the earth can set before us the state of grace for which we all hunger.

To my mother and father, Marjorie and Sidney Cleveland

In gratitude for all your love and support
and for letting me mess up the kitchen all those years

Acknowledgments

I thank God for my life and for the many blessings showered on me. One of them was the encouragement of many guests at the Ranch to write a cookbook. It has taken lots of time and lots of nudging, and I am deeply grateful to all who waited. I also wish to thank some of the people who helped me so much in the creation of this book:

❦ Aysha Griffin, whose infectious enthusiasm combined with her editing, marketing and publishing skills gave me the boost I needed to finish an often derailed project.

❦ Donna Bailey, whose drawings so enhance the pages of this book and will bring back happy memories to so many.

❦ Joel Wastell, whose patience with me and expertise with the computer made sense of my ramblings and made it possible for us to publish the book ourselves, a challenging but satisfying experience.

❦ Karen Leen, who entered all those names into the computer(!), sent out mailings and press releases, and performed dozens of other tiresome but necessary tasks.

❦ I also give thanks to the many other people who enrich my life and help me keep all the balls in the air at once:

❦ The Ranch kitchen staff, past and present, especially Pen Leng, Sokum Siek, Kathy Sevilla, Joan Nelson, Kymry Borkenhagen, Georgia Bostedt, Paulette Ross, Kathy Brazil, and Duke Gribble, who kept the Ranch fires burning (but never the food!), while I juggled kitchen duties, cookbook writing and baby raising. Without their daily support I never would have survived the last few years, let alone written a book.

❦ Other Ranch staff, especially Diana Rhoten, Dan Son, Cynthia Plattner, Edalee Dawson, Marci Westerbeke and Isabel Cogo who were all so helpful as my mind disintegrated throughout this baby and book creating process.

❦ The Westerbeke family, who took me into their beautiful home and their extravagant, generous hearts, gave me the freedom to create and the space to heal, and have continued to give me that freedom and space even as my life has evolved away from them. Someday may every business owner share Patty's vision of healing and service and may every working mother have an employer as supportive as Wendy has been to me.

❦ Virginia Farr, my spiritual mother, who so gently insisted that I speak my truth.

❦ Brother Jesse Gutierrez, who taught me I could know God with my heart, and Gil Bailie, who taught me I could love God with my mind.

❦ Robert Hoffman and the staff of the Quadrinity Institute who made the concept of loving myself into a real, day-to-day experience.

❦ My family in Texas, my parents, my brothers John and Mark, my sister Sarah, and my sisters-in-law, Kathy, Debbie and Lynne, who have loved me through the years and across the miles.

❦ My sons Zebi and Jesse, who expanded my culinary horizons to include ketchup on everything from cereal to ice cream, and are a constant reminder that life is fun and that we are all God's children.

❦ My husband Herman, who has nurtured my creativity as no other, kept me going when all seemed hopeless (ah, those 2 a.m. feedings!), taught me that anything is possible, and laughed with me as we have witnessed countless miracles.

I love you all.

Contents

Introduction *by Wendy Westerbeke* 5

A Note From Carol 7

Blessings 9

Bread & Breakfast 11

On the recipes 12

Soups 29

Why I Never Want to Work in a Restaurant 30

Hors D'Oeuvres 49

The Ranch Kitchen, Then and Now 50

Pasta 63

Salads and Salad Dressings 77

On Our Cooking Style 78

Poultry 99

Seafood 113

The Ranch Bell 114

Vegetables 127

Desserts 145

Do Your Best, Leave the Rest 146

Index of Recipes 193

Ranch History ....*inside back cover*

Abbreviations

c.	Cup	Tbl.	Tablespoon
tsp.	Teaspoon	lb.	Pound
oz.	Ounce	qt.	Quart

INTRODUCTION

We are delighted to present this cookbook from Carol's kitchen at the Westerbeke Ranch. It is a gift of love and nurturing – touched by Carol's skill, her heartfelt caring for our guests and the creation of delicious, wholesome meals. It is magic to me how all the food she touches tastes great. She claims that if I follow these recipes, I too can do that. What faith she has!

Past guests will rejoice at this publication. Year after year they trustingly signed their names to our cookbook registry, asking, begging for this chicken recipe, that salad dressing.

During the years that the cookbook has been in process, the Ranch has grown and changed. Our rustic redwood cabins remain perfect for overnight groups of 50 or less, while our meeting rooms can accommodate much larger groups. We have a marvelous new outdoor hot tub in a private area below the pool, and a new redwood deck enhances our garden area. Our massage studio provides a serene place for a relaxing massage from our professional staff. Every year, returning guests comment on how beautiful it is here at the Ranch. They notice the little changes and appreciate it as a home away from home.

Many of our new guests come to experience our latest offering: the Ropes Course. Built in the wooded creek canyon on our back 90 acres, this Outdoor Learning Experience, as we call it, is quite an incredible event for team and confidence building and enhancement of trust, commitment and communication. We hope to share this innovative facility with corporations and other groups of people who work/learn together, and who strive for success in the development of these human qualities.

The Westerbeke Ranch continues, as our brochure says, to be "A World Apart… for people who meet together." A wonderful eclectic mix of privacy, serenity, hospitality and exuberant creative growth, the Ranch is a special place for all sorts of conferences, gatherings and seminars. And, as you can see from this cookbook, the food is varied, healthful and delicious, thanks to the magic touch of Carol.

—Wendy Westerbeke
November 1991

*In sincerest gratitude
to Carol
for her many gifts*

A Note From Carol

I have always loved to cook, to feed people, but it wasn't until I was in my late twenties that I decided to make it my life's work. Then I went to cooking school in France and for a while I tried to be a "professional" in New York City. I couldn't do it. As the years went by I found that numbers and competition and self-promotion took the focus off of what was becoming increasingly important to me, which is that feeding people is a holy experience. And thus I came, as so many do, a spiritual refugee to California and to the Westerbeke Ranch. Here I found a safe haven where I could put into practice my newly hatched ideas about turning my chef's ego into a servant of the higher good. The Westerbeke Ranch was the perfect place for me in that respect because, being a conference center and not an eating center, I was in a secondary role from the start. Amazing work is done by people who come here for seminars and workshops. Daily I see individuals in incredible pain willing to face deeper pain in order to emerge healed and whole, teachers and school administrators using their creative energies to better serve their students, business people learning how to work together more efficiently, nurses and other healers finding new parts of themselves to use in helping others. In short, the people who come to the Ranch seek to make the world a better place, by healing themselves and through serving others.

It is inspiring to witness and a great satisfaction to be able to support these efforts through my cooking. Many people arrive at the Ranch in need of nurturing, others soon need it because of the difficult work they are doing here. To provide that nurturing is my job. I still put down "executive chef" on forms that ask for my occupation, but in a way that's the least important part of my work. Similarly, I feel that recipes are the least important part of cooking. Perhaps that's why it has taken me so long to write this cookbook. Every time I would start to accumulate recipes a part of me would quietly say no, this is not it. What I really want to communicate to people is that cooking is a way of giving, of connecting. Each of us yearns to find our connection to God, to feel we are living as we were meant to live. Life gives us so many opportunities

7

are living as we were meant to live. Life gives us so many opportunities to find that connection; too often we are not paying attention and miss them. But we can also choose to see the sacred in every moment of our lives, even something as mundane as making a pot of soup and sharing it. I know that cooking and eating are a basic expression of giving and receiving, the foundation of the sacred experience. Of course there are many difficult moments, times when I feel rushed, angry or frustrated while I am cooking. But my heart remains committed to the ideal, which is that each act in cooking is dedicated to service, to healing, to love. That is why I am so grateful to have found a home at the Westerbeke Ranch. The beautiful and tranquil setting is my greatest asset—it seems to open the hearts of all of us and to make possible the magical exchange of food lovingly prepared and received. And to everyone who has eaten my food and given me the gift of enjoying it I am also grateful.

Carol Cleveland Bojarsky
November, 1991

Blessings

Blessings on the blossom
Blessings on the fruit
Blessings on the leaf and stem
Blessings on the root

Lord, we thank Thee for Thy food
For health and home and all things good
For sun and rain
For skies above,
But most of all for those
We love

Bread & Breakfast

On the Recipes

Having spent the past few years stealing moments to write this book I have a new appreciation for cookbooks and their authors. It's hard work! And this is a tiny book compared to many—I'm in awe of the amount of effort represented by your average big cookbook, full of color photos, detailed index, and exhaustive background research.

It has been a challenge translating actions and ideas into numbers and words. I found myself struggling with several issues, not the least of which was the notion that putting a recipe in this book was somehow claiming it as "mine". Cooking is an art whose links to the past are fundamental; there is no such thing as a wholly original recipe. In a way a recipe is a kind of history—the one my mother sent me when I was living in my first apartment, the banana bread recipe from one of my college roommates, the secret shared by a chef from a favorite restaurant in Paris. And of course, many recipes originally came from other cookbooks. There are changes here and there, but even the ones that first saw life when I opened the refrigerator and had to make something with the six things I found there are inextricably linked to the bedrock that is our collective culinary culture. Fancy words, but I love the notion that I am part of the great circle, the eternal mother at the hearth, who turns an assortment of meats, vegetables, grains, whatever, into the stew of life that nourished my ancestors, and will nourish my great grandchildren.

As I began to record specific recipes, I inevitably had to deal with the fact that over the years I have developed a habit of cooking by instinct rather than numbers. This is mostly a survival strategy. Since the appearance of small people in my life, it seems like I'm always in a hurry. The more I can do by just remembering, or inventing, the faster I can move. Since we don't run a restaurant where patrons might return for the same dish over and over, I am concerned more with making sure things taste good each time they're made, but not necessarily that they taste the same every time. That's why a lot of recipes give ranges in quantities and most say "taste and adjust seasoning". I don't know how else to account for differences, shadings in flavor, evolution of taste and individual preferences. I hope anyone who feels cheated that I don't have everything pinned down to exact figures will return his or her copy for a cheerful refund.

Adjusting quantities was another challenge. I've scaled down most all the recipes to proportions most individuals will want to deal with, but there's a lot of grey here too. Actually, I think it works in favor of the scaled down recipe. After all, if you're focusing all your attention on the preparation of just one chicken, instead of twenty, or making one quart of soup instead of six gallons, it stands to reason that the smaller portions will get a more concentrated dose of that energy and come out better. Right? Makes sense to me.

The main point I want to make is that these recipes are the beginning, not the end. I hope to make changes up to the last minute before the ink goes on the paper, and if there are reprintings there will be more changes. The lovely thing about food is that it is perishable. You make it, you eat it and then it's gone. In talking to people about cooking I notice they get more pleasure reminiscing about hilarious disasters than recounting triumphs. It's a wonderful place to experiment, to experience failure, because no matter what happens there's nothing left the next day, except perhaps a tummyache. As my husband says, the worst thing that can happen is that you end up sending out for pizza.

Basic Bread Recipe

To make six loaves

6 c. water, 85°–95° (warm, not hot)
2 Tbl. yeast
½ c. honey
2 c. powdered milk, optional
6–8 c. white flour, in all
(unbleached bread flour is best)
8–10 c. whole wheat flour, in all
¾ c. vegetable oil
2 ½ Tbl. salt
6 c. rolled oats

I. SPONGE—Combine water, yeast and honey. Stir in about half of the flours to make a soupy mixture. Set aside in a warm place to rise for 15–40 minutes. This allows the yeast and the gluten to start developing before being weighted down by the rest of the ingredients. Even just a rest while you assemble the other ingredients will help.

II. MIXING AND KNEADING—Add salt and oil to sponge and fold in gently. Next stir in oatmeal. Start adding flour by the cupful. The proportion of white and whole wheat flour is up to you—less than one third white flour and the texture will get pretty heavy. After a while the dough will become too thick to stir. Turn dough onto a floured board or counter and begin kneading. To knead, lift end of dough farthest from you and fold over towards you. With arms straight and heels of hands against dough, push into dough, leaning into it with the weight of your body. Turn dough one quarter turn and fold and push again. Continue folding and pushing.

At first you will need to sprinkle flour on the board often to keep dough from sticking. Gradually though, the dough will come together and lose its stickiness. Add just enough flour to keep dough from sticking to board—too much flour makes for dry bread. After 10–15 minutes dough will feel elastic and smooth. Place dough in a large bowl, cover with a cloth and set in a warm place to rise. A sunny spot on a counter, an oven with a pilot light, or placing the bowl in another bowl of warm water will all work. The length of time dough takes to rise depends on the temperature of the air around it. Eighty to ninety degrees is ideal—warmer and the dough rises too fast and you risk exhausting the yeast. Colder and the dough takes a very long time to rise. Of course you can use this to your advantage if you need to leave the bread-making arena for a while. Just pop the dough into the fridge and you slow down the yeast. Then you can go away for several hours, even overnight.

In any case, the dough must now rise until it doubles in bulk. Besides a visual assessment, you can judge the dough's readiness by pressing the surface with two fingers. When the dough springs back in response to pressure, it's ready. At this point you may form the dough into loaves, but if you have time it's nice to give it a second rising. With a clean fist, gently but firmly push the dough down to press out the air—about 25–30 times. Cover with cloth and let rise again. The second rising will be faster, probably 45–50 minutes.

III. FORMING AND BAKING—When the dough is ready, turn it out onto a clean, lightly floured board. Cut the dough into 5 or 6 equal pieces. I like to weigh each piece for consistency's sake, and make my loaves 1 ½ pounds each, using the extra for a free form loaf or giving it to my son to create a fantasy bread. To form a loaf, take a ball of dough and knead it 5 or 6 times. Press dough into a rectangle about 9 inches by 5 inches and roll it up lengthwise. Pinch seam with fingers and press on loaf to flatten it a bit. Then place it in a greased bread pan and push dough to fill corners of pan. When all loaves are formed and in pans, make 2 or 3 slits about ¼" deep along length of loaves to allow them to expand more as they rise. Loaves may be brushed with beaten egg if a shiny crust is desired. Once more, set loaves in a warm place to rise for 20–30 minutes. Place in a 350° oven and bake for 55 minutes to an hour. To test for doneness, remove a loaf from the oven, tip it out of the pan and tap the sides with your fingernail. The crust will be, well, crusty and will sound hollow when tapped. When done, remove loaves from the pans immediately—if left in the pans they will get soggy. If humanly possible, let bread cool at least 20–30 minutes before slicing. It will slice more smoothly when cooled a bit, plus very hot bread is considered unhealthful for reasons I have been unable to track down. It figures though—it's the old "if it's delicious it must be bad for you " theory.

Notes About Bread Making

1. If you have doubts about your yeast, dissolve it in ¼ c. warm water and add a few teaspoons of honey or sugar. Let it sit for five minutes. If mixture has formed a bubbly foam on top, the yeast is active—proceed with recipe. If nothing has happened discard mixture and get some fresh yeast.

2. For extra richness part of the water may be replaced by eggs, and the oil by melted (and cooled) butter. The more butter or oil, the more tender the bread will be. More sweetener makes for a darker loaf.

3. Herbs, spices, nuts, grated cheese, chopped onion or garlic can all be added to bread dough with delicious results.

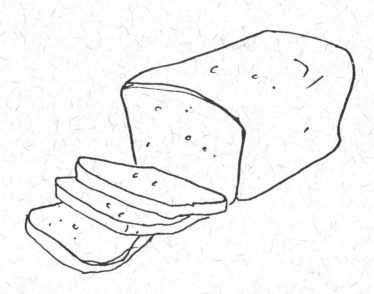

Challah

Twice a year I have the honor of preparing a giant loaf of challah for the shabbas service that opens the weekend retreats held at the Ranch by Congregation Sherith Israel of San Francisco. Rabbi David Meyer and his wife Marla are host to a wonderful two days of song, study and fellowship. It is a time when meals become more than just food; they are a symbol of community and our bonds with the past. It is always exciting to me to be a part of the celebration, and making a larger-than-life challah is a joy.

Note: This recipe will make quite a large loaf of challah (about 15 inches long and 8 inches in diameter). For a smaller loaf use one half or a third of the dough to form the challah and make regular loaves of bread with the rest.

3 c. eggs
  (12–16, depending on size)

3 c. water

3 Tbl. yeast

½ c. sugar or honey

14–16 c. unbleached white flour

2 ½ Tbl. salt

1 c. corn or other
  vegetable oil

1 egg beaten with

2 Tbl. water

poppy seeds

Follow general recipe for bread, using eggs and water for liquid.

After letting sponge rise, stir in oil and salt, then work in flour until stiff enough to knead. After kneading and rising, divide dough in 2 parts, one part ⅔ of dough, the other ⅓. Divide the larger section in thirds and, working on a floured surface, roll each piece into a rope about 15" long. Braid the three ropes, pinch ends together and place on a greased baking sheet. Repeat with the smaller portion of dough, dividing it in thirds, rolling into three smaller diameter ropes of the same length, and braiding the three. Brush the larger braid with the beaten egg and water. Sprinkle the top with a tiny amount of flour along the length of the loaf—this will make the two pieces adhere. Place the smaller braid on top of the larger one, pushing down gently but firmly to make sure it is securely attached. Brush all surfaces with beaten egg, then sprinkle with poppy seeds.

Let rise ½ hour (more if room is cold) then bake at 350° 1–1 ½ hours or until loaf sounds hollow when tapped and tester inserted well into center comes out clean. Let cool on a wire rack at least ½ hour before serving.

Challah makes the best French toast ever!

Whole Wheat Biscuits

⅞ c. white flour
2 tsp. baking powder
½ tsp. baking soda
2 tsp. sugar
½ tsp. salt
1 c. whole wheat flour
⅓ c. butter, grated
1 c. buttermilk,
  yogurt or sour cream

Sift together white flour, baking powder, soda, salt and sugar. Stir in whole wheat flour. Cut in butter with pastry cutter. *(Grating the butter helps incorporate it faster; grated frozen butter makes the fluffiest biscuits ever.)* Work in butter until pieces of butter are no longer visible and mixture is the texture of coarse meal. Pour in buttermilk and stir quickly. Turn onto floured board and knead lightly 5 or 6 times. Roll out to ½"–¾" thickness and cut in rounds or other shapes with a biscuit cutter (hearts are very nice). Or with knife or pizza cutter cut into squares—this saves time since there are fewer scraps to re-roll.

Place biscuits on a greased or paper lined baking sheet and bake at 375° 10–15 minutes or until puffed and brown. Serve hot.

Bran Muffins

Batter makes about 24 muffins and will keep in a sealed refrigerated jar up to 2 weeks, so muffins may be baked as needed.

1c. boiling water
½ c. oil
2 ½ t. baking soda
1 c. buttermilk
¾ c. brown sugar, firmly packed
2 eggs
¾ c. flour
¾ c. whole wheat flour
1 c. miller's bran
1 c. All-Bran
1 c. wheat germ
½ tsp. salt
1 c. raisins
1 c. chopped nuts

Combine water, oil and baking soda and let stand until lukewarm. Add buttermilk, brown sugar and eggs. In a separate bowl combine flours, bran, All-Bran, wheat germ and salt. Quickly stir dry ingredients into wet, stirring only until just moistened. Fold in raisins and nutmeats. Let stand at least 2 hours before baking. Spoon batter into greased or paper-lined muffin tins. Bake at 375° 20–25 minutes.

Apple Carrot Muffins

To make one dozen muffins

1 c. flour
½ c. whole wheat flour
1 Tbl. baking powder
½ tsp. cinnamon
½ tsp. salt
½ c. each chopped apple, raisins, grated carrot and chopped walnuts
¾ c. milk
½ c. brown sugar
¼ c. oil
2 eggs

Sift flours, baking powder, cinnamon and salt. In a bowl combine remaining ingredients. Add dry ingredients all at once and stir just until moistened. Overbeating makes muffins tough.

Pour into greased muffin tins and bake at 375° 10–15 minutes.

Blueberry Muffins

To make one dozen muffins

½ c. butter
1 c. sugar
2 eggs
1 tsp. vanilla
½ c. milk
2 ½ c. blueberries
2 c. flour
1 tsp. salt
2 tsp. baking powder

Sift flour, salt, and baking powder and set aside. Beat butter and sugar until light and fluffy. Beat in eggs one at a time. Add vanilla. Toss blueberries with 1 Tbl. of the flour mixture, then add flour and milk alternately by thirds to the butter mixture. Gently fold in the blueberries and spoon the batter into greased muffin tins. Bake at 375° for 15 minutes.

Banana Bran Muffins

To make one dozen muffins

1 egg
¾ c. brown sugar or honey
1 ⅓ c. mashed ripe bananas
½ c. walnuts
⅓ c. vegetable oil
1 tsp. vanilla
¾ c. flour
¾ c. whole wheat flour
½ c. oat bran
2 tsp. baking powder
½ tsp. baking soda
1 tsp. cinnamon
¼ tsp. salt

Combine egg, brown sugar or honey, bananas, walnuts, oil, and vanilla. Sift white flour, baking powder, baking soda, cinnamon and salt. Mix in whole wheat flour and oat bran, and add to wet ingredients. Stir until just mixed and spoon into greased muffin tins. Bake 15–20 minutes at 375°.

Cornbread

To serve six

1 c. cornmeal, yellow or blue
1 c. flour, white
or half white and half whole wheat
4 tsp. baking powder
1 tsp. salt
1 c. milk
1 egg
¼ c. oil
2 Tbl. honey

Sift flour, baking powder and salt. Stir in cornmeal. Mix together remaining ingredients and stir quickly into dry ingredients. Stir only until just mixed.

Pour into a greased 8"x8" baking pan or 12 muffin tins and bake at 400° until done, about 20–25 minutes for bread, 15 minutes for muffins.

Church Cornbread

Until motherhood changed the pattern of my life, I made this sweet, extra rich cornbread every Sunday for our meditation and healing service which has come to be known as the Community of Francis and Clare. Each week, an hour of laughter, tears and prayer ends with the sharing of bread and fresh juice. Preparing the bread for such a purpose is the sweetest way I know to begin a week.

To serve sixteen

2 c. flour
2 c. blue cornmeal
3 Tbl. baking powder
2 tsp. salt
½ c. brown sugar
2 ½–3 c. heavy cream
2 eggs
optional :
1 c. chopped nuts, raisins, blueberries

Sift dry ingredients, except for cornmeal, stirring it in. Add eggs and enough heavy cream to make a thick batter. Stir in optional ingredients and pour into a largish greased pan. I usually used a 10" heart pan. Bake 25–30 minutes at 400°. This bread is very tender and crumbly; treat it lovingly.

Jalapeño Cornbread

To serve six to eight

2 eggs, beaten
1 small can of creamed corn
1 Tbl. baking powder
1 c. sour cream
½ c. corn oil
1 ½ c. corn meal
1 small can jalapeños or 4 fresh
   jalapeños seeded and chopped
2 c. grated cheese

Mix all ingredients except jalapeños and cheese. Pour half of the mixture into a greased 8" square baking pan. Top with cheese and chilis, cover with remaining batter. Bake 30–35 minutes at 375°.

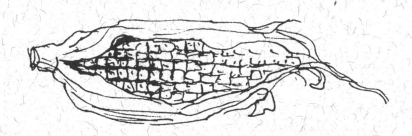

Spoonbread

Like polenta or tapioca, this corn pudding is wonderfully comforting.

To serve six.

1 c. cornmeal
2 c. boiling water
1 Tbl. butter
2 tsp. salt
1 c. milk
2 eggs, beaten
3 Tbl. sugar

Pour boiling water over cornmeal. Cook in a double boiler, stirring constantly, for five minutes. Add butter, salt and sugar. Let cool a few minutes, add milk and eggs, and beat for two minutes. Pour into a well-greased one quart deep baking dish. Bake one hour at 350°. Serve hot with butter.

Andy's Banana Bread

To make one 9" loaf

½ c. oil
1 c. sugar
2 eggs
3 mashed bananas
Juice of ½ lemon
2 c. flour
1 Tbl. baking powder
1 tsp. salt
1 tsp. cinnamon
1 c. chopped pecans or walnuts

Mix oil, sugar, eggs, banana and lemon juice. Sift together flour, baking powder, salt and cinnamon. Quickly combine dry and wet ingredients, stirring just enough to blend. Fold in nuts. Pour into a greased bread pan. Bake at 350° 50 minutes to one hour, or until toothpick inserted in center comes out clean. Let it rest 5 minutes, slide knife around edges and turn out on to a rack to cool thoroughly before slicing.

Banana Bread II

To make one 9" bread pan or one 9x13" pan

2 c. flour
1 tsp. baking soda
1 tsp. baking powder
1 tsp. salt
1 tsp. cinnamon
2 eggs
1 ¼ c. sugar
½ c. oil
1 tsp. vanilla
1 ¼ c. mashed ripe bananas
½ c. buttermilk
½ c. toasted and chopped walnuts
        or pecans

Sift flour, baking soda, baking powder, salt and cinnamon and set aside. Beat eggs, sugar, oil, vanilla and bananas. Stir in half the flour mixture, then the buttermilk, then the rest of the flour. Mix in walnuts and pour into prepared pan. Bake at 350° 45-50 minutes for bread pan, 30-35 minutes for sheet pan.

Buttermilk Coffeecake

To make 12 servings

2 ¼ c. flour
½ tsp. salt
2 tsp. cinnamon
½ tsp. ginger
1 ¼ c. brown sugar
½ c. white sugar
¾ c. vegetable oil
1 c. chopped walnuts or pecans
1 tsp. baking soda
1 tsp. baking powder
1 egg
1 c. buttermilk

Mix together flour, salt, 1 tsp. cinnamon, ginger, sugars and oil. When well combined, remove ¾ c. for the topping and add to the topping portion the nuts and the other 1 tsp. cinnamon. Set aside.

To the remaining mixture add baking soda, baking powder, egg and buttermilk. Stir to combine; don't worry about small lumps in the batter. Pour into a greased 9"x13" baking pan. Sprinkle topping over all. Bake at 350° 40–45 minutes.

Irish Soda Bread

To make one 8" round loaf

2 c. flour
1 ½ tsp. baking powder
½ tsp. baking soda
½ tsp. salt
1 Tbl. sugar
¼ c. butter
1 c. currants
2 tsp. caraway seeds
1 beaten egg
⅔ c. buttermilk

Sift dry ingredients. Cut in butter with a pastry blender. Stir in currants and caraway seeds. Add egg and buttermilk and stir briskly.

Knead briefly and press dough into a buttered 8" round baking pan. Cut a deep cross into the dough, brush with milk and bake at 375° 35–40 minutes.

Honey Orange Syrup

1 ½ c. honey
½ c. orange juice concentrate
1 tsp. cinnamon

Heat honey gently. Stir in orange juice and cinnamon. Adjust flavors to taste.

Serve with pancakes, French toast or waffles.

Granola

4 c. rolled oats
1 ½ c. coconut
1 c. almonds, chopped
1 c. sunflower seeds
½ c. flax seeds
½ c. sesame seeds
½ c. bran
½ c. vegetable oil
½ c. honey
1 Tbl. vanilla

Combine oats, coconut, almonds, sunflower, flax, and sesame seeds, and bran. Spread out on a baking sheet. Bake at 300° for one hour, stirring occasionally. Heat honey, oil and vanilla in a small saucepan until well blended. Pour over baked cereal, stir thoroughly and put back on baking sheet. Return to oven for 30 minutes.

Omelette Soufflé Roll

To serve eight

This is a most elegant brunch dish with the additional advantage that it can be prepared in advance and reheated. Many fillings lend themselves to this presentation. You will need 3–4 cups of filling. Chopped steamed broccoli folded into 2 cups of cheese sauce (pg. 123), cooked seafood in cheese or cream sauce (pg. 124) or cubed ham with sautéed mushrooms and onions in cream sauce are possibilities that come to mind. For extra lavishness, additional sauce or hollandaise sauce (pg. 121) may be served on the side.

Base

5 eggs, separated
1 ½ c. milk, scalded
4 Tbl. butter
5 Tbl. flour
salt to taste
pinch of cayenne pepper
1 c. parmesan cheese

Grease a 10"x15" baking sheet (with sides) and line with waxed paper or parchment. Grease pan again and dust with flour. Set aside.

Melt butter in saucepan; off the heat, whisk in flour. Cook over medium flame 2 minutes, stirring constantly. Off heat, add scalded milk.

Return to fire and cook 2 minutes after mixture comes to a boil. Season with salt and cayenne pepper. In another bowl, beat egg yolks a few seconds then add half the hot mixture. Beat well then add the rest.

In a large, very clean non–aluminum bowl, beat egg whites and a pinch of salt until they are stiff but not dry. Stir ⅓ of the egg whites into the milk and egg yolk mixture with ½ the Parmesan cheese. Gently fold in remaining whites.

Pour onto baking sheet and sprinkle with remaining cheese. Bake at 400° for 15 minutes or until puffed and brown. When done turn out onto a clean towel and peel off paper. Place another sheet of buttered paper over the roulade and gently roll up. Wrap in towel and let rest a few minutes. This allows the roulade to cool in a rolled shape so that when you fill and roll it again it won't crack or break.

To finish, unroll roulade, remove paper. Spread filling evenly over surface. Carefully roll up starting on a long side; the finished roll will be 15" long. To serve immediately, place in hot oven for 5 minutes. Otherwise wrap well in plastic wrap or aluminum foil; unwrap and reheat in oven to serve. Carefully slice roll into 1 ½" thick slices. Place on plate cut side down to show spiral of omelette and filling. Spoon a little optional sauce around roll, garnish as desired with parsley, broccoli florette or paprika.

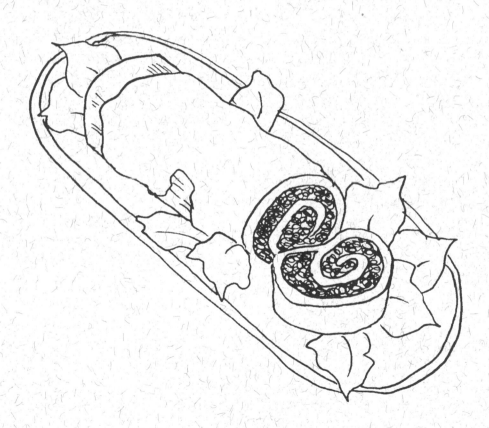

Soups

Why I never want to work in a restaurant

Many people assume that the goal of every cook is to own ones own restaurant. I guess it's true for many chefs. Certainly new restaurants open every day, but I can't think of anything I'd rather do less. When I eat at a well-managed restaurant that serves great food in a pleasing atmosphere, I give thanks to the person responsible as I would to a monk who has dedicated his life to the service of others. If you have never worked in a restaurant it is impossible to know the amount of hard work involved, the sacrifice of time and energy. One of the things I love most about my job is that it is possible to do it and live a somewhat normal life. Because we serve a single menu at each meal and meals are served at a specific time, working hours are reasonable. We finish dinner cleanup by eight or eight thirty, which is when things are just getting started in a restaurant. Of course, there's still weekend work, but through creative juggling and a great spirit of cooperation among staff members in the kitchen, we can almost always figure out a way for someone to have a weekend off when needed.

Another nice thing about preparing just one menu is that there are fewer surprises and less chaos in the kitchen. We start out the shift knowing just what has to be done and with a precise goal—to have the meal ready at the set mealtime. Of course there are surprises—lunch gets moved back half an hour, extra people suddenly arrive and need to be fed, but for the most part we can work steadily without the pressure of the eight o'clock rush, or twelve orders for twelve different dishes coming in at the same time.

Another thing I love about cooking at the Ranch versus a restaurant is that we are not dependent on liquor sales to make a profit. Not because food sales make a big profit—which seems impossible where you are serving quality food—but because the Ranch generates other income, particularly room rates, that help cover our operating expenses. Of course, we do serve beer and wine, and are happy to now be making a modest amount of money from that, but there is never the attitude that staff is expected to push alcohol sales. Even at weddings, where overindulgence is the social norm, we rarely see anyone drunk. It is refreshing, and hopeful, to see that people can gather and enjoy themselves without excessive alcohol. It is also much more gratifying for us in the kitchen to cook for people who we know have their senses about them to truly appreciate the food we serve.

And then, the greatest advantage of cooking at the Ranch versus cooking at a restaurant is that people have come there for another purpose than eating. Perhaps a big chunk of the credit for our reputation for great food goes to the surprise factor. How much lower can ones expectations be about the food to be served than when heading off to a seminar at a conference center located in the middle of nowhere?

I also give credit to the appetite-building factors of hard work, particularly brain work, and fresh air. Having been a participant in a few workshops myself, I know how often one emerges from a session of a few hours with the most enormous appetite. The sight of food incites joy, ecstasy, frenzy. Even guests who are not working find themselves eating as never before—the country air, they say.

Added to all of this is the lack of anxiety people so often experience in a restaurant—what do I order, how much does it cost, is there enough to eat, should I have ordered what my neighbor ordered. We have the advantages of a cafeteria—you can see what you're getting and take only what you want—without the steam table deadness of cafeteria food. And of course, unlike a restaurant, you can go back for seconds! My conscience stops me from offering seconds on dessert. I rationalize that although people might take more dessert if offered, their higher selves don't really want it. Maybe I'm doing them a favor by not tempting them twice.

One of my favorite books ever was *Dinner at the Homesick Restaurant* by Anne Tyler. One of the members of the family in the book takes over a very formal continental restaurant and gradually transforms it into what, for me, is the fantasy of what restaurants should be. He tears out the wall between the kitchen and the dining room. This was before kitchen as a stage became chic; the intent was literally to break down the barrier between the feeders and the fed. A bank of refrigerators on one wall of the kitchen was available for anyone to peruse and take what he needed. Motherly waitresses would assess the needs of each customer and recommend nurturing dishes. Prices were based on the means of individual diners. Ten years ago, when I first read this book, I felt it was just what we all needed. Now I am even more convinced that we are all "homesick". We all have a hungry heart, and the greatest thing I have to offer the people I cook for is the comfort of food prepared with love. In love there is a healing, a satisfying of the hunger that haunts us.

About Soup

Most recipes for pureed or cream soups have flour, arrowroot or other starch added as thickeners. This gives you more soup from less vegetable. Nutritionally this seems wasteful. I prefer to have the thickness and body of a soup come from the vegetables themselves or from potatoes or rice cooked with the vegetables if they are appropriate. This means using more vegetables in proportion to liquid but the resulting intensity of flavor is worth it. Also, after years of making soups with water instead of chicken or beef stock because of the numbers of vegetarians around these days, I now find I prefer the vegetarian versions—they taste more "vegetabley". These are not delicate, ethereally smooth French cream soups that result from straining out the fiber. They are hearty, no-doubt-about-it vegetable soups. Cream, butter or oil are still used—you just can't get around the flavor-enhancing quality of fat. But I usually make a non-dairy version as well or we offer sour cream on the side.

More hints on soup making:

• Leeks are more expensive than onions but they have a wonderful flavor and cook down to a silky texture for pureed soups.

• Add fresh herbs off the heat, just before serving.

• Remember, most commercial soups achieve their thickness from flour or other starch. They will start tasting more and more like glue as you get used to lighter, thinner soups.

• Add salt just before serving, after you've added liquids, etc. and go lightly—there's nothing more sad than a pot of otherwise delicious but too salty soup.

• To save aforementioned over-salted soups, add cream, milk, water, or pureed tomatoes or unsalted tomato juice, any kind of very watery vegetable that will cook quickly (spinach, lettuce or chard). If only a little bit too salty another strong flavor may counteract it—lemon juice , salsa (if not salty itself), for example.

• Lots of leftovers can be added successfully to soup: cooked rice, potato, pasta, vegetables, cooked meats.

Flavor enhancements to experiment with:

• Lemon or lime juice to bean soup, asparagus, broccoli or any soup that tastes "flat".

• Chopped fresh basil or cilantro, though the latter is a matter of individual taste. I could eat it all day long but some people do very uncivilized things when they unknowingly get some in their mouths.

• Oriental seasonings—sesame oil, tamari, fresh ginger.

Whenever you're unsure of what a particular seasoning will do to a soup put a small quantity in a bowl and try out the additions there. Remember to add tiny amounts at first.

If holding down calories and/or cholesterol are important to you, yogurt can be added to soup instead of sour cream.

Lite sour cream and yogurt must be added just at the end and the soup must not boil once they have been added.

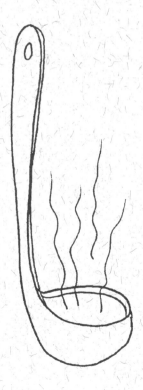

Basic Vegetable Soup

To serve eight to ten

½ c. butter

1 lg. leek, white part only,
  split lengthwise in quarters,
  washed well and chopped

3 lbs. vegetables: carrots, broccoli,
  cauliflower, spinach, sorrel, celery,
  celery root, potato, or combination
  of two or three, chopped

2–4 cloves garlic, if desired

water, vegetable or chicken stock

seasonings: salt, pepper, herbs
(see below for specific suggestions)

1 c. heavy cream, sour cream
  or yogurt

Sauté leek in butter 8 minutes or till soft and translucent. Add vegetable, dry herbs and garlic and sauté a few more minutes. Add enough liquid to just cover, bring to a simmer and cook till vegetable is soft. (If using 2 vegetables with different cooking times, i.e. potato and spinach, add the one that takes longer to cook 10 minutes before the other). Puree soup or puree half of soup and leave the rest chunky. Add cream or sour cream or yogurt, salt and pepper to taste, fresh herbs. If sour cream or yogurt is added, do not allow soup to boil again.

Broccoli-Cheese Soup: Add 2 c. grated cheddar or swiss cheese with cream.

Sorrel: Sorrel makes a delicious lemony spring soup. It turns brown when cooked, however, so you may want to add a bunch of spinach to green things up a bit.

Celery Root and Potato: This is a classic French combination that is delicious and perfect for cold winter days. Celery root has a delicate celery flavor and pureed, a hearty ribsticking texture.

Carrot Ginger Soup

To serve four to six

1 stick butter
1 large leek,
    white part only, chopped
8 carrots,
    peeled and roughly chopped
4 cloves garlic
water to barely cover
1" piece ginger, grated
lemon juice, salt, white pepper
chopped almonds, optional

Melt butter in soup pot and add leek. Saute until soft and translucent, then add garlic. Cook one minute, then stir in carrots and water to cover. Bring to a boil and simmer 20 minutes or until carrots are very soft. Puree in blender or food processor and return to heat. Just before serving add grated ginger and lemon juice, salt and white pepper to taste. Offer optional almonds and yogurt or sour cream on side.

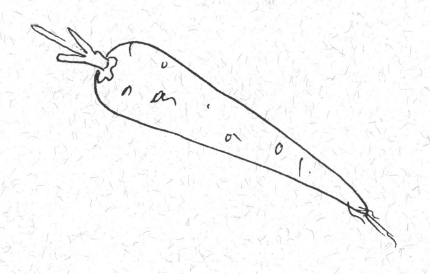

Red Chard and Potato Soup

To serve four to six

1 bunch red chard, washed and
   roughly chopped, stems included
3 Tbl. olive oil
2 leeks, sliced in quarters
   lengthwise and well washed
6 cloves garlic, peeled and sliced
½ tsp. red chile flakes
1 tsp. salt
1 lb. red potatoes,
   scrubbed and cut in ½ " cubes
2 tsp. nutritional yeast, optional
7 c. water or vegetable stock
sour cream

Sauté leek, garlic, and chile in olive oil until leek is soft. Add potatoes, yeast and water. Bring to a boil and simmer 5 minutes. Add chard, pushing leaves into the pot. Simmer 20–30 minutes. Eat as is or puree half of the soup—it should still have plenty of texture. Adjust seasoning, serve with sour cream on the side.

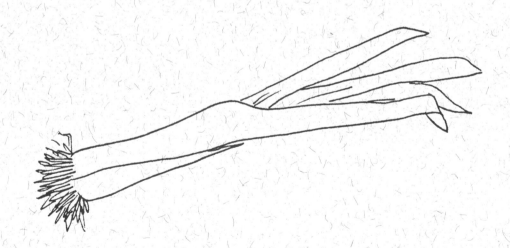

Onion Soup

The key to delicious onion soup is a long slow cooking of the onions, allowing them to slowly caramelize to a deep golden brown. All the salty beef broth in the world can't beat the richness of onions given their due.

To serve six

½ c. unsalted butter
2 Tbl. olive oil
6 lb. onions, finely sliced
2 tsp. sugar
water to cover,
    1 c. of which may be white wine
1 tsp. thyme
salt, pepper
optional garnish: slices of toasted
    French bread and
    grated Gruyere cheese
    or croutons and grated parmesan

Heat butter and oil in a heavy bottomed saucepan and begin sautéeing onions. Keep heat low so that onions soften, turn translucent, then begin to brown. It takes about 45 minutes to an hour for the onions to brown to a rich gold without burning. Sugar is added halfway through to enhance the caramelizing. When onions have had their time to brown, add water to just cover and thyme. Let simmer 30 minutes and adjust seasoning. Soup may be served in individual, oven proof bowls, topped with a slice of French bread and grated Gruyere and run under the broiler to melt cheese, or may be served with croutons and grated Parmesan on the side.

Potato Bacon and Cheese Soup

To serve six

¼ c. unsalted butter

2 onions, thinly sliced

2 lb. boiling potatoes, cubed

6 c. water or stock

¼ tsp. thyme

½ lb. bacon, fried crisp
   and crumbled

1 lb. cheddar cheese, grated

milk to thin

2 tsp. dry mustard

salt and pepper to taste

chopped chives for garnish

Sauté onions in butter until soft. Add potatoes, water or stock and thyme and simmer slowly until potatoes are soft, about 30 minutes. Puree half or all of soup, depending on desired texture. Add milk to thin to proper consistency and stir in mustard, bacon and cheese. Taste for seasoning, adding salt and pepper as needed. Do not let soup boil after adding milk. Garnish with chopped chives.

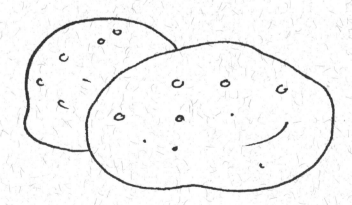

Pea & Spinach Soup

To serve six

1 stick butter
1 large leek, white part and 1"
   of green part, sliced in quarters
   lengthwise, chopped, and
   thoroughly washed
   or 1 large onion, chopped
1 tsp. curry powder
4 c. water
2 bunches fresh spinach, washed
   and roughly chopped
10 oz. pkg. frozen tiny peas
1 tsp. honey
salt, white pepper,
   lemon juice to taste
2 c. heavy cream or half & half

Sauté chopped leek or onion in butter till soft, about 5–6 minutes. Add curry powder, sauté a few moments then add spinach. When spinach is wilted add water. Bring to a boil and simmer 5 minutes. Add peas and honey and simmer another 5 minutes. Puree in blender or food processor, add cream or half & half and reheat gently. Season with salt, pepper and lemon juice.

39

Cream of Mushroom Soup

To serve six

2 sticks butter

2 large leeks, white part only, split lengthwise, chopped and thoroughly washed

8 cloves garlic, chopped

2 lbs. mushrooms, sliced or chopped in food processor or sliced by hand

1–2 tsp. dill, more if fresh

water or vegetable stock

1–2 c. heavy cream

salt, white pepper, lemon juice

Sauté leeks in butter till soft. Add garlic, mushrooms and dill (if using dried) and stir until mushrooms start to exude water. Barely cover with water or stock and let simmer 10–15 minutes, then puree. Add cream and reheat. Season with salt, white pepper, a squirt of lemon juice, and fresh dill if using.

Notes:

1. *When slicing mushrooms, unless a perfect slice is needed as for a crudité basket, cut a small slice off one side of mushroom, then place cut side on cutting board so that it won't slip away as you slice.*

2. *Garlic cloves can be peeled easily if first crushed with the broad side of a large chef knife or cleaver. Even if you're going to chop the garlic, crushing it first bruises the cells and releases more flavor.*

Curried Squash and Mushroom Soup

To serve six

2 lbs. squash , (butternut or banana
    squash are easiest to deal with)
    peeled and cut in chunks
water to cover
½ c. butter
1 leek, white part only,
    split lengthwise and chopped,
    or onion, chopped
3 cloves garlic, crushed and chopped
½ lb. mushrooms, sliced
1 tsp. ground cumin
½ tsp. ground coriander
1tsp. ground cinnamon
1 tsp. ground ginger
1 tsp. dry mustard
¼ tsp. cayenne
½ c. frozen orange juice concentrate
salt
lemon juice
garnish— chopped toasted almonds
sour cream or yogurt

Put chunks of squash in stock pot and cover with water. Bring to a boil and simmer till squash is very soft. Mash with potato masher or puree in blender or food processor, being sure to save all cooking water. Meanwhile, sauté onion or leek in butter till soft—about 5 minutes. Add garlic, mushrooms and spices and sauté till mushrooms are tender—about 10 minutes. Combine with pureed squash and its cooking water and orange juice. Reheat, correct seasoning, making it as spicy as you like. Add more orange juice or lemon juice to perk up flavors. Serve with almonds and yogurt or sour cream on side.

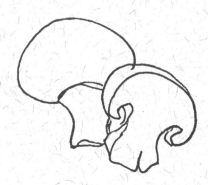

Minestrone Soup

To serve six

¼ c. olive oil

2 onions, sliced

8 cloves garlic, crushed and chopped

1 Tbl. basil

1 tsp. oregano

3 stalks celery, chopped

2 carrots, peeled and sliced

1 large sweet red pepper, chopped

2 zucchini, sliced

1 head cauliflower,
  cut in small flowerets

4 fresh tomatoes, chopped

1 large can tomato puree
  or crushed tomatoes

3–4 c. water

½ c. red wine

salt, pepper, fresh chopped basil

2 c. cooked garbanzo
  or kidney beans

1 c. dry pasta (elbows, for example)

Sauté onions in olive oil 5 minutes, or until soft. Add garlic and herbs and sauté 2 minutes, stirring constantly. Add celery, carrot, peppers and sauté 5 minutes. Add water, tomatoes, tomato puree and red wine, let simmer until vegetables are still crisp but beginning to soften—about 10 minutes. Add zucchini, cauliflower and pasta, simmer till all is soft. Add cooked beans, fresh basil, and more chopped garlic if desired, salt and pepper. Serve with a bowl of grated parmesan on the side.

Gaspacho

To serve six

1 cucumber, peeled

1 green or red pepper, seeded

3 fresh tomatoes

2 stalks celery

2 green onions, cut in ½" pieces

2–4 cloves garlic, crushed
and finely chopped

2 pieces stale French bread

6 c. tomato or V8 juice (in winter)
or

10 fresh tomatoes if real, homegrown
summer tomatoes are available

2 Tbl. red wine vinegar

2 tsp. honey

¼ c. olive oil

salt, pepper , lemon juice to taste

a few leaves fresh basil if available

a few dashes of tabasco sauce
if desired

Finely chop vegetables or finely chop half and puree other half in blender or food processor. Soak French bread in vinegar and tomato juice to cover and let soak till soft. Combine vegetables, seasoning, soaked bread, rest of ingredients. Taste for seasoning. Let chill several hours. Sour cream or yogurt and chopped chives or green onions may be offered on the side.

Curried Zucchini Soup

To serve six

¼ c. butter
2 onions, chopped
8 zucchini, approx 2 lbs., chopped
1 Tbl. curry powder
water
1 c. yogurt or sour cream
salt, pepper

Sauté onions in butter, until soft and translucent. Add zucchini and sauté 5 minutes more. Add curry powder, stir in to heat slightly, then pour in water to almost cover zucchini. Let simmer 10–15 min. or until zucchini is very soft. This soup may be puréed but I prefer to leave it chunky, just roughly mashing vegetables in the pot with a potato masher. Add yogurt or sour cream and heat gently. Do not let boil. Add salt, pepper, and additional curry powder if desired.

Split Pea Soup

To serve six

3 c. split peas
8 c. water
1 lg. onion, chopped
2 carrots chopped
2 bay leaves
1 ham bone or
   2 smoked hocks (optional)

Simmer all ingredients 1 ½–2 hours till peas are very soft and falling apart. Add more water if puree becomes too thick. Taste for seasoning and discard bay leaves and bones.

Baked Pumpkin Soup

A pumpkin, baked whole and served as the tureen for a soup made from its flesh makes for a whimsical presentation. A medium sized pumpkin (8") is best since larger ones may collapse during baking. Or baby pumpkins or acorn squash may be used for individual servings. If using the small squashes cook some extra to be sure to have enough pulp.

To serve eight

1 8" pumpkin,
4-6 c. water, vegetable or
   chicken stock, boiling
1 chopped onion
½ c. butter
1 bay leaf
½ tsp. thyme
1 c. heavy cream
roasted pumpkin or sunflower seeds
chopped parsley

Carve a lid from the top of the pumpkin, making sure it will be wide enough for your soup ladle to dip into the pumpkin later. Scoop out and discard the seeds and stringy fiber. You may roast the seeds to use as a garnish later.

Place pumpkin on a baking sheet or baking dish. If pumpkin does not seem secure make a collar of aluminum foil to put around its base to stabilize it. Add water or stock, butter and herbs to pumpkin. Place in a 350° oven and bake until pumpkin flesh feels soft when pierced with a fork (test by removing lid and testing from the inside— you don't want to make a hole in the skin of the pumpkin.) Remove bay leaf. Scrape flesh of pumpkin from walls leaving enough, about ½", to support the weight of the pumpkin. If the pumpkin flesh is very stringy you may want to scoop it out and puree it. Add cream and salt and pepper to taste. Replace cover and bring your prize to the table.

Ratatouille Soup

To serve six

2 medium eggplants
4 zucchini
2 sweet red peppers
1 lg. red onion
2 red tomatoes fresh or
    canned (in winter), chopped
water to cover
2 bay leaves
1 Tbl. basil
6 cloves garlic, crushed and chopped
salt and pepper

Cut eggplants, zucchini, peppers and onions in half, brush with olive oil and place on baking sheets, cut side down. Place in a 450° oven and bake till vegetables are soft. Remove from oven and chop roughly. In soup pot sauté in ¼ c. olive oil the garlic, basil and bay leaves. After 4 minutes add chopped baked vegetables, tomato, and water to barely cover. Let simmer 20-30 minutes. Puree in blender or food processor. Adjust seasonings with salt, pepper. Serve hot with a spoonful of saffron mayonnaise.

Saffron mayonnaise

1 egg
2 Tbl. lemon juice
    or red wine vinegar
4–6 cloves garlic,
    crushed and peeled
½ tsp. salt
1 Tbl. Dijon mustard
1 pinch saffron (approximately
⅛ tsp. dissolved in 1Tbl. hot water)
1 c. olive oil
¼ tsp. cayenne pepper, optional

Place egg, mustard, vinegar or lemon juice, garlic, salt, saffron and cayenne in blender or food processor. Cover and let machine process for one minute, pouring olive oil in a thin stream till mayonnaise thickens. Taste, and add salt or vinegar if needed.

Borscht

I was shocked to learn from a Russian friend that in its native tongue borscht promises soup, not necessarily even having beets. It can be cabbage soup, it can have meat in it, there are countless variations. With apologies to Tania I just can't shake the notion that borscht is beets, and cold to boot. My husband told me of a much loved borscht recipe at a restaurant where he worked in which the secret ingredient was ketchup. Some day I may try it on my ketchup-loving three year old, but I doubt it.

To serve six

2 lbs. beets,
    small and sweet preferred
4 c. water
1 tsp. salt
1 cucumber, chopped fine
½ c. chopped green onions
2 c. buttermilk
1 Tbl. chopped fresh dill
2 tsp. honey
fresh ground pepper to taste
sour cream on the side

Scrub beets well and cook in water and salt until tender. Save liquid, set beets aside until cool enough to handle. Slip off skins and grate beets coarsely. Return to cooking liquid and add remaining ingredients. Chill well.

Serve with sour cream.

Hors D'oeuvres

The Ranch Kitchen, Then and Now

Muriel Van Hoosear, my mother, and her good friend Marge Welcome, were noted for their gelatin-moulded fruit salad mandalas with cottage cheese on the lower level and Sunday roast legs of lamb (if they had arrived at the market) with frozen peas. Mother's Lady Baltimore cake with boiled raisin nut icing was a great hit.

Then, for 10 years we enjoyed a culinary reprieve, thanks to Mr. Takishima, a superb chef who had survived the humiliation of being dragged off to an internment camp after Pearl Harbor.

Following his departure, and under great protest, Diane Cobb and I were recruited to take over cooking when the seminar groups began to arrive. My best efforts were a six-bean casserole and a beef stroganoff over rice, both extremely complicated dishes made from cans, and a chicken dish smothered in grated cheese and crumbled potato chips. To make matters even worse, these were prepared at at our home in Mill Valley and brought to the Ranch for re-heating. Susie Westerbeke and Gary had a turn at a great many breakfasts, and Wendy washed a lot of dishes. Other cooks came and went. It is a testimony to the beauty of the Ranch and the goodness of our guests that they endured our cooking, and even returned again and again.

You can imagine our joy when Carol Cleveland finally took up the challenge. She came from Paris and New York and other points east, seeking a home and family and place to nurture and serve through her cooking. Here she met her husband and now has two sons and a lovely home.

Carol's expertise, coupled with her loving spirit, has transformed our Ranch kitchen, nourishing our bodies and souls. The compilation of this cookbook has been a labor of love. May these recipes not only enrich your palate, but your everyday life, and that of those whom you serve in love.

Patty Westerbeke
November 1991

Salsa Cruda

To make three cups

8 tomatoes
1 bunch cilantro
4 green onions
2–4 cloves garlic
1–4 jalapeños
1 tsp. salt
juice of one lemon or lime

Chop and combine ingredients, adding chiles one at a time until desired hotness is achieved. Salsa will keep 1–2 days if refrigerated.

Salsa Cocida

To make three cups

8 tomatoes
1–4 dried chiles de arbol
1 medium onion, chopped
¼ tsp. each clove, nutmeg, cinnamon
   and cumin
(salt to taste)

Drop tomatoes in boiling water for 30 seconds. Remove and peel. Chop finely or puree in food processor. Toast chiles in dry frying pan or directly over flame if you have a gas stove until the chiles brown and pop. Chop or grind by hand or machine and add to tomatoes with other ingredients. Simmer 10–15 minutes. Adjust seasoning, let cool. Salsa will last 1 week if refrigerated, for many months if canned and properly processed (follow canning jar directions for processing stewed tomatoes).

Salsa Verde

To make two cups

2 cans whole tomatillos
1 bunch green onions, chopped
4 cloves garlic
2–4 chiles, jalapeños or serranos
1 tsp. salt

Place all ingredients in blender or food processor and puree. Start with smaller number of chiles and taste before adding more.

Guacamole

Guacamole often has mayonnaise or sour cream added to it to mellow it or stretch it. Avocados are so rich in oil themselves they don't need added oil or butterfat. If thinning or stretching is desired try yogurt—it works like sour cream without weighting down the final product.

To make two cups

4 perfectly ripe avocados
2 Tbl. lemon juice
½ c. salsa verde
½ c. yogurt, optional
salt to taste

Cut avocados in half and scoop out flesh, discarding any dark portions. Mash with a fork or wire whisk (please, no cuisinarting). Stir in remaining ingredients and adjust seasoning. If salsa verde is unavailable substitute 1 clove crushed garlic and 2 chopped green onions.

Layered Bean Dip

For a 1 ½ qt. flat serving dish, ideally glass and about 3 inches deep.
To serve ten to twelve

2 c. refried beans or 2c. cooked beans, mashed and seasoned with cumin, oregano, salt, and Tabasco
2 c. guacamole
3 medium tomatoes, chopped
1 c. sour cream
1 c. salsa
¼ c. chopped cilantro

Spread ingredients, in the order listed, one layer at a time, in the serving dish. Chill up to one hour before serving. Serve with tortilla chips.

Salmon Seviche

To serve eight

½ lb. salmon filet
½ c. lime juice
1–2 jalapeños, chopped
½ tsp. salt
2 medium tomatoes, chopped
½ chopped cilantro

Slice salmon on the diagonal in ¼ inch slices. Cut each slice in pieces; ½ x 2" strips is a good size for spearing with a toothpick. Place in a glass or stainless steel bowl and add lime juice, salt and chilis. Stir, cover and refrigerate 8 hours to overnight. Before serving add tomatoes and cilantro.

Snow Peas Stuffed with Smoked Salmon

To make 50 hors d'oeuvres

½ lb. snow peas
4 oz. smoked salmon (I buy the salmon trim- much less expensive)
8 oz. cream cheese
1 tsp. lemon juice

Trim off the stem end of snow peas. Drop in boiling water 30 seconds then plunge in cold water. Drain peas and lay on a towel to dry. With a small sharp knife slit open the snow peas along one edge. Set aside. In blender or food processor puree salmon and cream cheese. Season with lemon juice. Refrigerate mixture briefly—you want it to be firm enough to hold its shape when piped without being too stiff to pass through the tip of the pastry tube. Place salmon mixture in a pastry bag fitted with a star tip. Holding a pea open with one hand pipe salmon along the length of the inside of the pea. If you are proficient with a pastry tube you can pipe decoratively with the tip in a scallop or loop pattern. Carefully lay each snow pea on its side on a tray and fill remaining peas. Keep refrigerated until served. May be made 2–3 hours ahead of time.

Makis

To make about fifty appetizers

½ lb. thin sliced Prosciutto
   or rare roast beef (you need 9 slices)

1 lb. goat cheese

1 bunch chopped fresh dill

1 red apple chopped in ¼" cubes,
   skin left on

1 cucumber, seeded and chopped
   in ¼" cubes, skin left on

1 red bell pepper, seeded and
   chopped in ¼ " cubes

2 English cucumbers, cut in ¼" slices
   or 50 2" rounds of thin sliced bread

Lay out 3 slices of meat, overlapping them slightly. Spread with ⅓ of the goat cheese. You should have a surface about 6"x8". Starting at the end nearest you lay out horizontal rows, first of apple, then cucumber, bell pepper and dill, gently pressing into the cheese. Roll into a log, starting from the edge nearest you. Wrap in plastic wrap and refrigerate at least 1 hour. Repeat with remaining ingredients. When ready to serve, cut with a very sharp knife into ½ " slices and place on a slice of cucumber or round of bread.

Ginger Pineapple Chicken

To make 50 appetizers

1 ½ lb. boneless chicken breast,
   cut in 1 inch cubes

2 Tbl. each soy sauce and sherry

¼ c. shredded ginger

4 cloves garlic, chopped

2 Tbl. oil

1 fresh pineapple,
   cut in 1 inch chunks

Marinate chicken in soy sauce, sherry, ginger and garlic for 2 hours. Sauté in oil in a very hot sauté pan or wok about 2 minutes or until just done. For a buffet dish skewer pieces of chicken alternately with pineapple on 6 inch wooden skewers. As an hors d'oeuvre skewer one piece each of chicken and pineapple on a toothpick.

Alternatively, raw marinated chicken and pineapple may be put on skewers (if wooden soak first for an hour in a bowl of water) and grilled over coals.

Chicken Liver Mousse

This recipe was given to me by a pastry chef I apprenticed with in Paris. It's a typical French heart-stopper, both in terms of its melting, velvety texture and delicate taste, and its ability to up all major arteries instantaneously with its cholesterol and saturated fat content.

To serve ten to twelve

1 lb. chicken livers
4 shallots, chopped fine
4 Tbl. unsalted butter
¼ c. cognac or very good brandy
salt, pepper
¼ lb. unsalted butter
½ c. heavy cream,
   whipped till stiff peaks form

Sprinkle livers with salt and pepper and sauté with shallots in 4 Tbl. butter until shallots are soft and livers are still pink inside. Pour on cognac and ignite. When flames go out set pan aside to cool. Puree mixture in food processor or blender. Beat in softened butter by the tablespoonful, then fold in whipped cream. Correct seasoning with salt and pepper. Chill before serving. Serve in a crock garnished with parsley and cornichons.

Wendy Westerbeke, 1953

Bagna Cauda

Bagna cauda means hot bath in Sicilian. I know heavy cream and butter sound rather decadent for a vegetable dip, but with the powerful seasoning of anchovies and garlic you need just the tiniest bit to add an intense kick to your crudités.

To make one cup dip

2 c. cream
4 Tbl. butter
8 anchovy filets, chopped
1 Tbl. chopped garlic

Reduce cream in half by boiling gently in a saucepan. Melt butter in a small saucepan and add anchovies and garlic. Sauté a few minutes and add cream. Serve hot with raw vegetables and bread-sticks.

Biscuit Sandwiches

This is a hearty hors d'oeuvre, the kind to serve at an appetizers-only party. They're also good for picnics, children's parties and tea parties. I like to make them with heart shaped biscuits—of course I've been known to make everything heart shaped from tofu burgers to wedding cakes.

To make twelve sandwiches

1 recipe whole wheat biscuits, to which you can add
1 Tbl. chopped fresh dill and 2 Tbl. chopped chives
Possible fillings:
    smoked chicken with mayonnaise and cranberry relish
    Roast beef with mayonnaise and horse radish
    Westphalian ham and sweet/hot mustard
    Curried Tuna (pg. 95)

Caponata

2 lb. eggplant,
   peeled and cut in 1 inch cubes

3 onions, chopped

4 stalks celery, chopped

2-6 cloves garlic,
   peeled and crushed

½–1 c. olive oil

1 lb. tomatoes,
   fresh or canned, chopped

¼ c. capers

¼ c. raisins

¼ c. pignoli (pine nuts)

½ c. red wine vinegar

1 Tbl. sugar

1 tsp. each salt and pepper

Sauté eggplant, onions and celery in ½ c. olive oil until vegetables are soft, about 15 minutes. Add additional olive oil as needed to keep vegetables from sticking. Add garlic and sauté another 2 minutes. Stir in tomatoes, capers, raisins, and pignoli, then simmer 15 minutes. Add vinegar, sugar, salt and pepper, then simmer another 10 minutes. Let mixture cool and refrigerate at least 2 hours before serving, preferably overnight. Serve with French bread or raw vegetables, or as a part of an antipasto tray.

Mushroom Piroshki

To make 24 pastries

1 recipe Cream Cheese pastry
  (pg. 131)
1 lb. mushrooms, chopped
4 shallots or 1 onion, finely chopped
1 clove garlic, finely chopped
4 Tbl. unsalted butter
1 Tbl. vegetable oil
½ c. sour cream
1 tsp. dried or 1 Tbl. fresh dill
salt and pepper
½ c. fresh bread crumbs
1 egg yolk
1 Tbl. water

Sauté mushrooms, shallots, or onion, and garlic in butter and oil until soft and mushrooms have exuded their liquid. Add sour cream, dill, salt and pepper to taste. Add enough bread crumbs to make a stiff mixture that will hold its shape if formed into balls.

Roll out pastry ¼ " thick. With a small knife or pizza cutter, cut sheet of dough into 3" squares. With a small spoon or pastry bag put a spoonful of mushroom filling in the center of each square. Place the egg yolk and water in a small bowl and whip a few seconds with a fork. With a pastry brush, spread a thin line of egg yolk around the edges of the pastry squares. With each square draw the four corners together in the center and pinches the edges together to form a small pouch of pastry. Place each one on a baking sheet and keep refrigerated until ready to bake. Brush pastry with egg yolk and bake at 375° 15 minutes or until pastry is puffed and golden. Serve right away. Pastries may be frozen baked or unbaked. If unbaked, place in oven directly from freezer and bake at 375° 20 minutes. If frozen already baked, reheat in a 375° oven 5-10 minutes or until heated through.

Roquefort Butter

This makes a nice canapé, as below, or may be rolled into a cheese ball. For a cheese ball all, or part, of the butter may be replaced with cream cheese.

½ lb. roquefort
or other very good blue cheese
(We use Oregon Blue)
½ lb. unsalted butter, softened
½ c. walnuts,
   finely chopped (optional)

Combine all ingredients. If serving as a cheese ball, roll in chopped parsley.

Roquefort Radish Canapés

The combination of the spikey hot of the radish and the creamy salty roquefort is much more delicious that it sounds. It also makes a very pretty hors d'oeuvre.

2" rounds cut from thin sliced
   white or pumpernickel bread
Roquefort butter
Radishes, cut in thin slices
tiny sprigs of parsley

Spread bread rounds with roquefort butter. Lay three overlapping slices of radish on the cheese and garnish with a sprig of parsley.

Tomato Pesto Canapés

This is one of my favorite flavor combinations—basil and tomato. These are also the ideal canape because they're so easy to put together, especially if you have frozen pesto on hand. They're also colorful and appealing for a buffet or hors d'oeuvres tray.

To make 50 hors d'oeuvres

Loaf of baguette size French or sourdough bread, cut in ¼" slices

1 c. homemade tomato paste or ¾ c. canned tomato paste combined with ¼ c. tomato sauce

½ c. pesto sauce

grated Italian cheese

Spread round of bread with tomato paste. Put ½ tsp. pesto sauce in the center of the round. Sprinkle lightly with cheese and serve.

Almond Pâté

To serve four as a main dish, eight as an appetizer

1 large onion, chopped
4 Tbl. oil
1 large clove garlic, chopped
½ tsp. cumin
½ tsp. dill
½ tsp. chervil or thyme
1 c. raw almonds, finely ground
½ c. bread crumbs, toasted
2 Tbl. chopped parsley
1–2 tsp. tamari or soy sauce
salt and pepper
2–4 Tbl. sour cream or mayonnaise
lemon juice
parsley and lemon slices for garnish

Sauté onion in oil 5 minutes or until soft and transparent. Add garlic and herbs and cook another 2 minutes; do not let vegetables brown. Scrape into a bowl and combine with almonds, bread crumbs, chopped parsley and tamari. Add sour cream or mayonnaise until mixture holds together. Season to taste with salt, pepper, and lemon juice. Refrigerate at least one hour before serving; flavors improve overnight. Serve in a crock garnished with parsley and lemon slices or form into a ball and coat with chopped parsley. As a luncheon dish we roll it in individual balls and coat with parsley and serve with fresh bread and assorted raw vegetables.

Pasta

Marinara Sauce

We make this sauce by the gallons. By varying the amount of liquid and seasoning it can be a simple sauce for pasta, the base for additives like fish and seafood, pizza sauce, lasagna sauce, a flavorful addition to vegetable soups, cream sauces and salad dressings.

2 onions, chopped

¼ c. olive oil

6 cloves garlic (or more), chopped

1 bay leaf

1 Tbl. basil

1 tsp. oregano

1 tsp. marjoram

1 tsp. thyme

2 28 oz. cans whole tomatoes,
     chopped or pureed in blender

1 8 oz. can tomato sauce

1 6 oz. can tomato paste

1 c. red wine

salt, pepper

2 tsp. honey

Sauté onion in olive oil until very soft. Add garlic and herbs and saute 2 minutes more. Add tomatoes, sauce, paste and wine and bring to a simmer. Reduce heat to low and cook 1–2 hours. Season with salt and pepper and add honey if necessary to balance the acidity of the tomatoes and wine.

Note: I always thought my husband added too much honey to his tomato sauce until I stopped drinking wine when I was pregnant. Then I realized the honey is necessary; if you're not drinking wine as a balance the acidity of the sauce is too much. So, it might be best to taste your sauce along with whatever you plan to drink with it. Of course one might make the same recommendation for any dish before seasoning.

Pesto Sauce

To serve eight to twelve

2 large bunches basil (about 1 lb.)

¾ c. olive oil

4–8 cloves garlic

1 tsp. salt

1 c. grated Italian cheese
  (I prefer half Parmesan
  half Romano)

½ c. pine nuts or walnuts

Pick leaves off basil stems, discarding black spots and flowers. Wash and dry leaves. Place leaves in bowl of blender or food processor. If they don't all fit at once fill bowl and add the rest later while machine is running.

Add garlic, salt and olive oil and start processing, adding more leaves as mixture purees and decreases in volume. Taste sauce; if it tastes bitter don't worry—adding more olive oil, 2 Tbl. at a time, will dilute the very powerful taste of the basil. Add nuts and process for just a few seconds to chop the nuts. Remove sauce to a bowl and add the cheese. Taste and add more salt if necessary.

For Pasta al Pesto toss the sauce directly on hot cooked pasta. This recipe will make enough sauce for about 2 pounds of pasta. Serve with extra cheese on the side.

If pesto is to be frozen, puree the basil with salt and half the amount of olive oil. Place in freezer containers and cover with a film of olive oil. Add garlic, nuts and cheese to the sauce when it is to be used.

Pasta Oopla

This is a recipe given to me by a chef at a restaurant in Rome called, as you might guess, Oopla.

To serve four to six

1 lb. rigatoni or other tubular pasta
1 c. each, marinara or tomato sauce
pesto sauce
heavy cream
Grated Italian cheese

Cook pasta in large quantity (4 quarts per pound of pasta) of salted boiling water. While pasta is cooking heat tomato sauce and cream in a saucepan and boil down a few minutes to thicken slightly. When pasta is cooked, drain and add to sauce. Stir in pesto sauce and serve immediately. Do not cook sauce after adding pesto sauce. Serve with grated cheese on the side.

You can play around with the proportions of the three ingredients in this sauce, using less cream or pesto as your diet and taste allow. It's good almost any way, even with no cream at all for the truly virtuous.

Lasagna

A few years ago I happened to notice a recipe on a box of lasagna noodles for Easy Lasagna. It turned out you can make lasagna without precooking the noodles— you just add some water to the tomato sauce and bake it an extra half hour. It was one of those tips that open up new highways of culinary adventures. Suddenly lasagna was in my grasp as a practical dish to prepare in a short time. Spur of the moment lasagna—the perfect buffet dish becomes more perfect!

For one 9"x13" lasagna pan

½ lb. lasagna noodles

2 qts. tomato sauce plus 1 c. water

2 lb. ricotta cheese

1 c. Parmesan cheese

4 eggs

½ c. fresh chopped basil

salt, pepper

1 lb. mozzarella cheese, grated

Options for fillings:

    1-2 lb. sweet Italian sausage, cooked and crumbled

    2 eggplants, sliced, brushed with olive oil and baked until soft

    2 lb. spinach, blanched, squeezed dry and chopped

    1 lb. mushrooms, sliced and sautéed in olive oil

    1 lb. zucchini, sliced and sautéed in olive oil

Combine ricotta with eggs, Parmesan, basil and season with salt and pepper. Spread about 2 c. tomato sauce over bottom of lasagna pan. Cover with noodles. Leave about ¼" between noodles; they will expand as they cook. Top with ½ of the ricotta mixture, ½ of the optional ingredients, ⅓ of the mozzarella and cover generously with tomato sauce. Repeat. Cover with a third layer of noodles and tomato sauce. Make sure noodles are completely covered with sauce. Cover with aluminum foil and bake at 350° one hour or until noodles are done—test by piercing with a small knife. Add more sauce as needed to keep top layer of noodles from drying out. Remove cover , sprinkle remaining cheese over all and return to oven 10 minutes. Let lasagna sit 10-15 minutes before cutting and serving.

A delicious addition, especially with vegetarian lasagna, is a tablespoonful of pesto sauce on each serving, spooned on just before serving.

Spaghetti alla Carbonara

To serve four to six

1 lb. spaghetti or other pasta
½ lb. pancetta or bacon
3 eggs
½ c. Parmesan cheese
salt and pepper

While spaghetti is cooking fry the pancetta or bacon until crisp. Cut into ½" pieces. In a bowl large enough to hold pasta when cooked, beat the eggs and add cheese, salt, pepper and bacon pieces. A little bacon grease or cream may be added if desired. When pasta is done, quickly drain and add it to bowl. Toss with two forks. You should see small clumps of cooked egg clinging to strands of spaghetti. If mixture seems to slimy for your taste, you may put mixture over the fire a few seconds to cook the egg a bit more, but don't overcook and dry out the eggs. Serve with extra cheese on the side.

Pasta alla Putanesca

This is one of the quickest pasta dishes to make—everything can be put together while the pasta is cooking. That's how it got its name, the idea being that prostitutes have to be able to make fast meals between tricks; the fact is, everyone needs to know how to make delicious meals this quickly. The quantities given here are approximate—increase, decrease or eliminate as you wish. Recently I added hot pasta to a bowl of fresh tomatoes, basil, garlic, olive oil, grated cheese and a dollop of Paul Newman's Italian dressing. It was one of the best pasta dishes I've ever eaten. (Of course, I was camping and extremely hungry!)

To serve four to six

1 lb. fusilli, rigatoni
    or other hearty pasta
¼ c. olive oil
2–6 cloves of garlic,
    peeled and crushed
4 Tbl. capers, roughly chopped
4 Tbl. Italian olives,
    pitted and chopped
4 ripe tomatoes, chopped
2 Tbl. anchovies, chopped, optional
1 c. fresh chopped basil
1 c. Parmesan cheese, grated

Bring a large pot of salted water to a boil and add pasta. At the same time prepare other ingredients and place them in a serving bowl. When pasta is cooked drain it well and add to bowl. Stir well to combine ingredients and serve.

Gorgonzola Pasta

This pasta is very rich but so delicious. And so easy—by the time the pasta is finished cooking everything can be ready to go.

To serve four to six

1 lb. linguine or other pasta
½ lb. gorgonzola
   or other very creamy blue cheese
½ c. cream or butter
1 c. walnuts, finely chopped
½ c. parsley, chopped

Add pasta to a large pot of salted boiling water. While it is cooking, mash cheese with the cream or butter until very smooth. Stir in walnuts and parsley. When pasta is done quickly drain and add to cheese mixture. Toss with two forks to melt and distribute sauce. Season with freshly ground pepper.

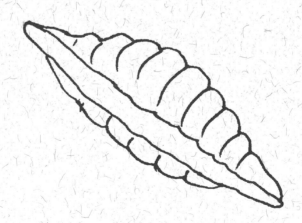

Linguini with White Clam Sauce

A waiter at my favorite restaurant in Rome shared this recipe with me. I'm afraid I didn't show my gratitude as he'd hoped I would, but I do think of him whenever I make Linguini con Vongole. This was the first time I had encountered the concept of finishing the cooking of the pasta in the sauce in which it is being served—a wonderful idea that I have tried with many other pasta dishes, always with delicious results.

To serve four to six

1 lb. linguini or other dry pasta—
   fresh will not work in this recipe

2 dozen live clams,
   rinsed and scrubbed

¼ c. olive oil

4–6 cloves garlic, thinly sliced

⅛ tsp. crushed red pepper

1 c. dry white wine

Cook pasta in 4 quarts of salted, boiling water, but remove pasta 2 minutes before it is done—it will feel almost tender, but still be hard at the very center. While pasta is cooking heat the olive oil in a large sautée pan with a tight-fitting lid . Add the garlic and sautée until just golden. Add the wine and when it boils add the clams. Cover the pan and let simmer until clams open. Remove clams, letting all liquid drain back into pan. Cover clams and keep warm. When pasta has reached the almost done point, drain and add pasta to the sautée pan with the crushed red pepper. Continue cooking until the pasta is done, about 3-5 minutes. Return the clams to the pan and reheat a few minutes. Serve immediately. Note: we Americans tend to put grated cheese on anything pasta; an Italian would never ever eat seafood pasta with cheese. Try it without; add cheese if you must.

Lobster Pasta

Pasta dishes offer an affordable way to treat oneself, and one's guests, to luxury items. This will still be an expensive dish, but how else could you ever feed six people with one lobster?

To serve six

1 ½ lb. pasta, linguine or similar
1 2 ½ lb. lobster
  (one lobster
  that weighs 2 ½ lb., that is)
1 bottle white wine
1 carrot, chopped
1 leek, white only, chopped
1 stalk celery, chopped
1 bay leaf
½ tsp. thyme
handful of parsley
½ tsp. salt
1 tsp. whole peppercorns
½ lb. butter
1 c. cream
lemon juice
optional vegetables, steamed—
    peas, mushrooms, tomato, etc.

Make a court bouillon by boiling wine with the chopped vegetables and herbs 15 minutes. Add the lobster and steam until just done, about 20–25 minutes. Remove meat from shells and set aside. Break up shells and return to the stock with the butter. Reduce until the liquid has evaporated and only the butter remains. Strain the butter through a sieve, pounding on the shells to remove all possible juice. Boil pasta 2 minutes less than usual—until it is almost done with a touch of hardness at the very center. Drain and place in saucepan with the lobster butter and cream. Cook until pasta absorbs the liquid. Season to taste with salt and lemon juice. At the last moment add the cut up lobster meat and tamalley, toss gently to reheat, and serve. Optional vegetables may be added for color.

Lemon Pasta

This is one of those recipes that I tried because I just couldn't believe it could work. Pasta cooked in gin? Impossible. Actually the original recipe called for vodka but that seemed pointless since vodka has no taste. It turned out to be a great dish, and one that lends itself to many variations.

To serve four to six

1 lb. pasta (dry not fresh)
1 c. cream
¼ c. lemon juice
grated rind of 1 lemon
¼ c. gin
½ tsp. salt
freshly ground pepper

Start pasta cooking in a large pot of boiling salted water. While it is cooking, assemble remaining ingredients. When pasta is 2 minutes from being completely cooked remove it from the heat and drain. It should be almost tender with just a tiny bit of hardness at the center.

Return the drained pasta to a saucepan and add remaining ingredients. Cook over medium heat until pasta absorbs most of the liquid in the pan and tastes done. Add more salt or lemon juice as needed. Stir in optional ingredients and serve immediately.

Optional additions:

3–4 oz. smoked salmon, cut in small pieces

6 oz. cooked fresh salmon

1–2 c. steamed vegetables; peas, zucchini, carrots are all good

Baked Polenta

I realize polenta is not a pasta, but I included it in this section as a reminder of what a great alternative to pasta it can be. The idea takes getting used to; the first time someone suggested it, I said no way to cornmeal mush under my spaghetti sauce. Once tasted, however, polenta creates lots of converts, especially among lovers of comforting, homey food.

The other off-putting aspect of polenta is the usual method of cooking—dribbling the polenta into boiling water, stirring vigorously and continuously for the 20 or 30 minutes it takes to cook, all the while on the alert for the errant lumps that seem to form no matter how diligent you are. The prospect of preparing polenta for 50 always daunted me until I found directions one day for baked polenta. I've never done a side by side taste test, so I can't assert that this is just as good as the long-stirred method; however, I feel safe in stating that more people will enjoy polenta more often when made this way.

To serve four

1 c. polenta

3 ¼ c. hot water
(we find we need 4 c. water with our convection oven—more evaporation, I guess)

1 tsp. salt

2–4 Tbl. butter

Generously butter a 1 ½ qt. baking dish with some of the butter. Add cornmeal, salt and the hot water; stir gently. Cover with tight fitting lid or aluminum foil. Bake 50 minutes at 350°. Remove lid, stir butter into mixture and bake another 10 minutes, uncovered, or until polenta is cooked and of a creamy consistency. Add more water if it's too thick. Polenta can be served instead of spaghetti with tomato or cream sauces or by itself with butter, cheese or sour cream, or all three.

Spicy Peanut Sauce for Noodles

To serve three to four

1 lb. Oriental noodles
   or fine egg noodles
2 tsp. sesame oil
1 c. smooth peanut butter,
   natural style preferred
6 Tbl. tea or hot water
4 Tbl. hot oil, optional
6 Tbl. tamari or soy sauce
6 Tbl. red wine vinegar
4 tsp. honey
salt to taste
2 Tbl. sesame oil
½ c. oil
2–4 Tbl. chopped garlic

Cook noodles according to package directions, but omit salt. When cooked, drain and rinse under cold water. Drain and toss with 2 tsp. sesame oil. To make sauce, place peanut butter and water, or tea, in a blender, or food processor, and blend until smooth. Add remaining ingredients and process until smooth. Add to noodles and toss to coat. Garnish with chopped fresh cilantro. Shredded cooked chicken (½ lb.) may be added.

Salads and Salad Dressings

On our cooking style

I feel the kind of cooking we do at the Ranch is ideally suited to "modern life". With rare exception we prepare everything for a meal, including salad, dessert, and setting the table, within two hours of serving. Translated to smaller quantities for one family, most meals can be prepared by one person in an hour or less. Occasionally dishes that require more time, stews or lasagna for example, also lend themselves to large quantity preparation and saving portions for future meals. Because we so frequently have guests on special diets, many of our dishes adapt readily to accommodate food preferences. We usually cook chicken and fish plain, by portion, and offer a sauce on the side. This works well at home for children with picky appetites or family members on a diet. I feel our menus reflect the style of eating people are aiming towards these days: big fresh salads, delicious vegetables, wholegrain breads, very little red meat and lots of meatless meals. Where we fall away from the straight and narrow path of lowered fat and cholesterol, (i.e. eggs for breakfast, lots of dairy, rich desserts), we try to offer an alternative for those who are farther along on their dietary evolution. One can choose fruit and yoghurt instead of eggs for breakfast, salad and steamed vegetables instead of cheese, whole wheat bread instead of buttermilk biscuits, fruit instead of chocolate cake.

As I serve at the buffet table I constantly witness the struggle created by such choices. I feel the ambivalence within myself of wanting to support people in their intent to choose health and to eat healthy food and, at the same time, knowing that most people love rich foods, particularly desserts. Personally, I love to delight the child in each of us with something sweet and delicious. A glance at the table of contents of this book tells you how I feel about dessert: it's a large chapter. It is a struggle that will stay with us, I suspect, until we make a choice to be conscious about what we eat. What we eat becomes us, and has a enormous influence on how well we feel, how our organ systems function and how well we can cope with stress, illness and disease.

But eating is also about joy, fantasy, creativity, love, giving and receiving, which don't pay any attention to facts like cholesterol or complex carbohydrates. My three year old was as excited today about the cherry tomato he picked himself from our garden as he was about the jiffy pop popcorn or the choclate ice cream bar. We talk to him about nutrition and what's good for his body, but he knows what's really important: the joy.

I see the type of food we serve at the Ranch as being without a dominant philosophy, except to celebrate all of the pleasures of eating: fresh tomatoes and basil right out of the garden, as well as the chocolate mousse cake. Some people find our meals the healthiest food they have ever eaten; for them it's a new experience to eat fresh fruit salad for breakfast, green salad for lunch and dinner, fresh vegetables and fish. Other people treat themselves while at the Ranch and indulge in the desserts, cheeses, and breads they restrict in their everyday life. Others are quite firm about sticking to a particular diet they have adopted. And there are people in between, changing from day to day, meal to meal. And although it can be frustrating to have the person for whom you have just prepared a lowfat, non dairy, complex-carbohydrate complete-protein vegetarian meal announce, "Tonight I think I'll have the chicken," I say hurrah! As Jesus said, it is not what goes in your mouth that counts, it's what comes out of it.

I believe there is room for all of us at the table. Perhaps we can worry less about what we eat in terms of saturated fats, calorie tables and eating animals. More attention might be given to how that vegetable or animal was raised, how much it was adulterated in getting to market, and with how much care it was handled in the kitchen. We try to buy the best raw materials, though only about half of our food is organic at this point. Through much of the summer, and some of the spring and fall, a lot of our produce comes from our own garden or from the farmers market here in town. Even the produce that comes from the wholesale markets has been personally purchased by the buyer at our local grocery store. Our eggs, too, come from a farm just down the road. While I sometimes have to compromise because of cost or convenience, the closer I get to the source, the better I feel. The ideal is when I am the only "middle man" between the grower and the Ranch guest. I've strayed from that ideal many times, as my staff could detail, trying to make life a little easier. I still wince at the commercial mayonnaise experiment, avocado frozen in a can or the "pure maple syrup" that turned out to be only 5% maple.

We're still learning.

Basic Vinaigrette

We make salad dressings in a food processor because the powerful mixing of the machine's blades creates a very smooth emulsion of liquid and oil. Since we serve salads undressed and the bowl of dressing sits on the buffet throughout the meal, it helps to have a dressing that won't separate—the last person in line gets the same dressing as the first. For smaller quantities, or if you're going to dress your salad before serving it (the way salad is meant to be served), emulsified dressing isn't such a necessity.

⅓ c. wine vinegar
½ tsp. salt
2 tsp. Dijon mustard
¼ tsp. white pepper
1 c. olive oil

Place first four ingredients in blender or a jar with a lid. Process or shake vigorously to combine. Pour in oil with machine running or add oil to jar and shake again.

Variations:

Mustard Dill—increase mustard to ¼ c. and add 1 tsp. dill
Curry—add 1 tsp. curry powder
(Curry powder added to apple dressing is also very good.)
Garlic—add 1–4 cloves crushed garlic
Herb—add 1 tsp. dried or 1 Tbl. fresh chopped herbs
(tarragon, thyme, chervil)
Blue cheese—add ½ c. crumbled blue cheese

Orange Vinaigrette

To make 1 cup

⅓ c. frozen orange juice concentrate
⅓ c. white wine vinegar
1 clove garlic
½ tsp. salt
¼ tsp. white pepper
1 tsp. dry mustard
½ c. vegetable oil

Put all ingredients, except oil, in bowl of blender or food processor. Blend one minute then pour in oil in a slow stream. Taste and adjust seasonings.

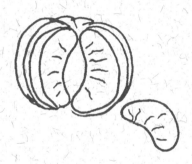

Orange Yogurt Dressing

This is a tangy light salad dressing that is particularly refreshing in the summer. It can be a good nonfat dressing by eliminating the mayonnaise and using nonfat yogurt.

To make 1 cup

⅓ c. frozen orange juice concentrate
½ c. yogurt
3 Tbl. mayonnaise
squeeze of lemon juice

Combine all ingredients in a small bowl. Whisk until smooth. Taste and add more orange juice concentrate if desired.

Sesame Orange Dressing

To make two cups

1 c. orange juice
¼ c. white wine vinegar
1 Tbl. soy sauce
2 Tbl. sesame oil
½ tsp. salt
1 tsp. dry mustard
½ tsp. dill
1 clove garlic
½ c. light vegetable oil

Place all ingredients, except oil, in blender or food processor. With machine running pour in oil. Taste and adjust seasoning.

Tarragon Mustard Dressing

1 egg
⅓ c. Dijon mustard
¼ c. tarragon vinegar
1 tsp. dried tarragon
salt, pepper
½ c. olive oil
½ c. vegetable oil

Put egg, mustard, vinegar, tarragon, salt and pepper in bowl of food processor or blender and process 1 minute. With machine running pour in oil in a thin stream. Taste and adjust seasoning.

Honey Mustard Dressing

To make two cups

½ c. apple cider vinegar
¼ c. Dijon mustard
¼ c. whole grain mustard
¼ c. honey
½ tsp. salt
1 ½ c. light vegetable oil

Place all ingredients, except oil, in blender or food processor. With machine running pour in oil. Taste and adjust seasoning.

French Dressing

To make two cups

2 eggs
½ c. red wine vinegar
¼ c. sugar or honey
1 Tbl. dry mustard
½ tsp. salt
1 tsp. paprika
1 c. oil

Combine eggs, vinegar, sugar or honey, mustard, salt and paprika in blender. Process for a few seconds then start pouring in oil in a thin stream. Taste and adjust seasonings.

Apple Cider Dressing

To make one cup

⅓ c. frozen apple juice concentrate
⅓ c. apple cider vinegar
1 clove garlic
1 tsp. dry mustard
½ tsp. salt
½ tsp. white pepper
½ c. oil

Place all ingredients, except oil, in bowl of blender or food processor. Start machine, and after 30 seconds, begin pouring in oil in a thin stream. Taste and adjust seasoning.

Poppy Seed Dressing

To make two cups

1 egg
2 Tbl. sugar or honey
1 Tbl. Dijon mustard
⅓ c. red wine vinegar
½ tsp. salt
2 Tbl. finely chopped onion
1 c. light vegetable oil
1 ½ Tbl. poppy seeds

Place egg, sugar or honey, mustard, vinegar, salt and onion in blender or food processor. Turn on machine and slowly pour in oil. Stir in poppy seeds. Taste and adjust seasoning.

Avocado Dressing

To make one cup

1 perfectly ripe avocado
1 clove garlic, crushed
1 Tbl. lemon juice
1–2 drops Tabasco sauce
buttermilk to thin, about ½ c.

Scoop out flesh from avocado and place in blender or food processor with garlic, lemon juice, salt and Tabasco. Process until smooth. With machine running pour in buttermilk until it reaches desired consistency. Taste and adjust seasoning.

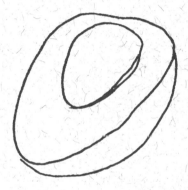

Salsa or Gaspacho Dressing

Salsa or gaspacho by themselves make a flavorful low calorie dressing. Or you can stir in a little mayonnaise to tame the taste a bit. Or you can add a greater proportion of mayonnaise, whir the whole thing in the blender and achieve a more refined dressing though the taste will never be subtle. But then, we've never been known here at the Ranch for subtlety in our salad dressings.

Red Barn Dressing

I have no idea why this dressing has this name. It's one of hundreds my mother, a dedicated recipe clipper, has sent me over the years that has become one of my standbys. Besides the great taste what I love about it is the ridiculous number of ingredients.

To make three cups

2 c. mayonnaise

1 avocado

6 green onions, roughly chopped

½ small can anchovies, rinsed

¼ c. buttermilk

1 tsp. Tabasco

1 ½ tsp. Worcestershire sauce

1 ½ tsp. tamari or soy sauce

1 ½ tsp. wine vinegar

¼ c. lemon juice

¼ tsp. each: celery seed, dry mustard, oregano, white pepper

1–2 cloves garlic, peeled

Combine all ingredients in blender or food processor, and purée until smooth.

Lemon Parsley Honey Dressing

To make one cup

1 bunch parsley, stems removed
juice of 2 lemons
2 cloves garlic, crushed
2 Tbl. honey
½ tsp. salt
½ c. olive oil

Place all ingredients, except oil, in blender or food processor. Run machine a few minutes to finely chop parsley and garlic. With machine running pour in oil in a thin stream. Taste and adjust seasoning.

Garden Dip

To make four cups dip or spread

2 c. mayonnaise
8 oz. cream cheese, softened
1 bunch each, watercress,
    radishes and scallion
2 Tbl. mustard
salt and pepper

Wash and roughly chop vegetables. Then fine chop in food processor. Beat cream cheese until smooth, then stir in mayonnaise, vegetables and mustard. Add salt and pepper to taste. Refrigerate 1 hour or more to develop flavors. For a sandwich spread use 1 c. mayonnaise.

Mayonnaise

As if eggs didn't already have enough of a bad name, now we're not supposed to eat them raw for fear of salmonella. I feel you have to go by your instincts about the food you eat. The eggs I eat at home come from our own chickens. The eggs at the Ranch come from our friendly egg ranchers, Kathy Karr and Terry Province, down the road. Their chickens are raised in a healthy, free environment, and fed the best food possible. I feel totally confident about eating such eggs; I wish everything we ate could be as pure. Even made in the food processor, homemade mayonnaise is such a treat that I offer the recipe and leave it to you to decide if you trust your eggs.

We make our mayonnaise in the food processor—it's fast, foolproof and uses whole eggs instead of just yolks. Making it by hand is almost as easy, however, as long as you remember that although you do have to beat constantly, you don't have to wear yourself out beating fast—slow and steady does just fine.

To make one and one-half cups

1 egg (2 egg yolks if hand made)
1 Tbl. wine vinegar or lemon juice
½ tsp. salt
2 tsp. Dijon style mustard
1 c. oil, may be part olive oil

Place all ingredients, except oil, in blender or food processor. Start machine and process 1 minute. With machine still on pour in oil in a thin stream. Taste and adjust seasoning depending on application; as a dressing for salads with a bland base, such as potato or pasta, you want the mayonnaise to have extra oomph (in the form of lemon juice, salt and pepper—see also additions to mayonnaise).

For hand-made mayonnaise, start whisking egg yolks, vinegar, lemon juice, salt and mustard. Start pouring in oil drop by drop. About halfway through adding the oil you will notice you are over the hump—the mixture has achieved the emulsion state. At this point you can pick up the tempo—the droplets can become a thin stream. Remember, with mayonnaise the more oil you add the thicker it will be.

Additions to mayonnaise

Green Mayonnaise—a wonderful dip for artichokes or crudités

Add any or all of the following to the mayonnaise ingredients before processing:

2 green onions, roughly chopped

½ c. chopped parsley

2–3 Tbl. fresh herbs, basil, chervil, tarragon, dill

2–3 cloves garlic, peeled

Saffron Mayonnaise—great for seafood salad or with Ratatouille Soup

big pinch of saffron threads, soaked for 10 minutes in 1 Tbl. boiling water

2–4 cloves garlic

1 Tbl. fresh basil, optional

Patty Westerbeke, circa 1939

Potato Salad

To serve six to eight

2 lbs. potatoes, red or white
¼ c. dry white wine
1 Tbl. red wine vinegar
1 Tbl. lemon juice
1 Tbl. Dijon style mustard
2 cloves garlic, crushed and chopped
¼ tsp. salt
6 Tbl. olive oil
1 tsp. pepper, freshly ground
3 green onions, chopped
2 stalks celery, chopped
3 Tbl. chopped parsley

Scrub potatoes and boil in salted boiling water until they are just tender. Drain, and when they are just cool enough to handle, cut them in ¼ inch slices, (they may be peeled—we never do), and place them in a mixing bowl. Sprinkle with the white wine and toss very gently. Set aside and prepare dressing. Beat vinegar, lemon juice, mustard, garlic and salt in a small bowl with a wire whisk. Beat in oil in a thin stream. Season to taste—dressing should be tart to wake up potatoes. Pour over potatoes. Add pepper, onions, celery and parsley and stir gently to mix all ingredients. Salad may be served warm or at room temperature. If it has been refrigerated, let it warm up at room temperature 30 minutes before serving. Taste for seasoning just before serving—potato, rice and pasta salads seem to lose their zing when they sit in the fridge a while; a fresh infusion of lemon juice or salt and pepper can quickly bring them back to life.

Hot Potato Salad with Sausage

To serve six

2 lb. boiling potatoes, red or white
1 lb. sweet Italian sausage,
   pork or turkey
1 red onion or
   3 green onions, chopped
½ c. chopped parsley
2 stalks celery, chopped
½ lb. fontina cheese, cut in ½ " cubes
⅓ c. apple cider vinegar
salt, pepper

Boil potatoes in salted water until tender. When cool enough to handle cut in 1" chunks. Sauté sausage until cooked, then cut in ½" slices. Add sausage to potatoes with onion, celery and cheese. Sprinkle with vinegar, salt and pepper to taste and toss thoroughly. Add parsley and serve immediately. If not to be served hot, omit cheese.

Rice Salad

I give a recipe here, but you can really put just about anything in a rice salad. The rice itself can be leftover, as well as the vegetables, cold chicken, fish, turkey, meat, Chinese food, just about anything.Similarly just about any dressing is good, or a mixture of dressings.

1 c. brown rice, cooked in 2 c. water
    and cooled
    (or 2 c. leftover cooked rice)
1 cucumber, peeled and chopped
1 tomato, chopped,
    or 1 c. cherry tomatoes, quartered
3 green onions, chopped
2 stalks celery, chopped
1 c. peas, cooked and cooled
1 red bell pepper, cut in ½ " squares
3 Tbl. lemon juice
½ c. olive oil
salt and pepper

Combine rice and vegetables and toss. Sprinkle with lemon juice and oil and toss again. Season to taste with salt and pepper.

Curried Rice
with Cashews and Raisins

To serve six to eight

2 c. long grain brown rice
1 onion, chopped
2 Tbl. olive oil
1 Tbl. curry powder
1 tsp. salt
½ c. raisins
1 c. roasted cashews

Wash rice. Sauté onion in oil a few minutes and add rice. Stir and saute a few more minutes to coat brown rice. Add curry powder and stir to incorporate. Add water, raisins and salt. Stir once and cover. When water boils reduce heat to lowest simmer and cook until rice is tender. Just before serving stir in roasted cashews.

Wild Rice Salad
with Oranges and Pecans

To serve six

1 c. wild rice, cooked as for rice
    in 4 c. water and cooled
3 oranges, peeled and sectioned
1 c. pecans, toasted and chopped
¼ c. raspberry or rice vinegar
1 bunch watercress,
    large stems removed
salt and pepper to taste

Combine all ingredients and season to taste. I don't add oil to this salad—I guess the pecans and the wild rice give it enough richness, but some could be sprinkled on at the end if desired.

Tabouleh Salad

To serve six

1 c. bulgur
1 ½ c. boiling water
1 tsp. salt
¼ c. lemon juice
¼ c. olive oil
2–4 cloves garlic, chopped
½ c. chopped green onions
1 bunch parsley, chopped
1 cucumber, chopped fine
1 large tomato, chopped
½ c. chopped fresh mint

Pour boiling water over bulgur, stir well and set aside to soak and cool. When cool sprinkle with salt, lemon juice, olive oil and garlic, toss well and refrigerate 1 hour or more. Just before serving add remaining ingredients. Taste and adjust seasoning.

Red Cabbage Salad

For six to eight servings

1 small head red cabbage
salt and pepper to taste
½ c. chopped parsley
¼ c. red wine vinegar
½ c. olive oil
1 ½ c. toasted walnuts, chopped
4 oz. Roquefort or other
    crumbly style blue cheese

Finely shred cabbage and place in serving bowl. Heat vinegar to a boil and pour over cabbage and toss—the cabbage will brighten in color. Add parsley, salt and pepper to taste and olive oil. Toss again. Add walnuts and crumbled blue cheese. Toss and serve; may be chilled briefly before serving.

Curried Tuna Salad

When the tuna boycott began I switched to making this salad with chicken or turkey breast, which is also very good. Now that "dolphin safe" tuna is available we have a choice, and it's nice to have tuna again.

To serve four

1 7 oz. can tuna, drained
½ c. chopped apple, skin left on
¼ c. chopped celery
2 Tbl. almonds, toasted and chopped
1 Tbl. currants or raisins
1 Tbl. coconut
¼ c. curry mayonnaise

Combine all ingredients, breaking up chunks of tuna with a fork.

Curry Mayonnaise

2 c. mayonnaise
¼ c. curry powder
2 Tbl. chutney

Combine ingredients in a blender and process until smooth.

Chinese Chicken Salad

To serve four to six

1 lb. boneless chicken breast

1 Tbl. soy sauce

1 tsp. five spice powder

1/4 lb. mushrooms, sliced

1/4 lb. snow peas, stemmed

1 red bell pepper, cut in strips

1/4 lb. bean sprouts

2 stalks celery, chopped

1/4 c. red wine vinegar

2 Tbl. honey

2 Tbl. soy sauce

2 cloves garlic

1 inch piece of ginger,
    peeled and roughly chopped

2 Tbl. sesame oil

½ c. oil

Place chicken breast in a saucepan and cover with cold water. Add soy sauce and five spice powder and bring to a boil. Reduce heat and simmer 5–10 minutes or until just cooked. Let cool in pan. Drop snow peas into boiling water, remove after 30 seconds and immediately plunge in cold water. Drain and set on a towel to dry. To make dressing put vinegar, honey, soy sauce, garlic and ginger in bowl of food processor or blender. Puree 1 minute or until garlic and ginger are finely chopped. With machine running pour in oils. Cut cooled chicken in chunks or shred with fingers and place in a mixing bowl with the vegetables. Pour dressing over all and toss to mix. Let marinate 30 minutes before serving. If holding longer, add dressing to chicken and mushrooms. Add remaining ingredients just before serving.

Shrimp Salad with Grapes

To serve six

1 ½ lb. bay shrimp, cooked
2 c. celery, chopped
2 c. seedless green grapes
4 green onions, chopped
½ c. fresh dill, chopped
1 c. sour cream
1 c. mayonnaise

Combine shrimp, celery, grapes and green onions. In a small bowl combine sour cream, mayonnaise, and dill. Fold into salad. Season with salt and pepper. Refrigerate 2–4 hours before serving.

Jícama Orange Salad

This salad is of Mexican origin but goes well with any spicy meal.

To serve six

1 lb. jícama
2–3 naval oranges
1 bunch watercress
1 pomegranate, optional
2 Tbl. white wine vinegar
2 Tbl. oil
salt, pepper

Peel jícama with a sharp paring knife, being sure to peel away the fibrous layer underneath the brown skin. Cut jícama in ½ " cubes. Cut away the peel of the oranges, including the white part under the skin, and separate them into sections. Wash watercress and remove large stems. Open pomegranate and separate seeds. Toss all together, sprinkle with vinegar and oil and season to taste with salt and pepper.

Poultry

DonnaBailey 91

Barbeque Sauce

To make one quart

¼ c. oil
2 onions, finely chopped
6 cloves garlic, finely chopped
4 c. ketchup
¼ c. red wine vinegar
¼ c. soy sauce
¼ c. molasses
2 Tbl. dry mustard
1 tsp. cayenne pepper or to taste
1 Tbl. Worcestershire sauce
1–2 Tbl. liquid smoke (optional)

Sauté onion in oil 5 minutes. Add garlic and sauté 2 minutes more. Add remaining ingredients and simmer 30 minutes. Taste and adjust seasoning. This sauce will keep several months in refrigerator. Because of the molasses it will burn if put on meat at the beginning of a barbeque. I usually cook the chicken, or whatever, about half way then start brushing on the sauce. If baking in the oven, sauce may be put on at the beginning of cooking.

Caribbean Chicken

I love simple recipes and this is among the simplest, even if you sample the rum along the way.

For each chicken, cut in pieces,
¼ c. each:
    lime juice
    soy sauce
    Meyer's dark rum

Combine ingredients and pour over chicken. Let marinate 6 hours to overnight. Grill over hot coals.

Mexican Grilled Chicken
with Lime Marinade

To serve four

1 chicken, cut in serving pieces
   and skinned
½ c. lime juice
1 c. chopped cilantro
1 tsp. salt
1 tsp. oregano
1 tsp. cumin
½ tsp. cayenne
2 cloves garlic
3 Tbl. honey
¼ c. olive oil

Combine all ingredients except chicken and process well in blender. Pour over chicken and let marinate 6 hours to overnight. Grill over hot coals until just cooked, basting frequently with marinade. Note: chicken is skinned because the honey in the marinade makes it burn easily; removing the skin helps reduce the chances of the coals flaming up and burning the chicken. It helps to use a covered grill. If chicken still browns too rapidly, cooking may be finished in the oven. This all sounds kind of troublesome, but it's worth it—this is a delicious marinade.

Chicken Teriyaki Marinade

For each chicken:
1/4 c. soy sauce
1/4 c. frozen orange or
   pineapple juice concentrate
1/4 c. white wine
1/4 c. white wine vinegar or
   cider vinegar
4 cloves garlic, chopped
2 Tbl. shredded ginger

Combine all ingredients and pour over cut up chicken. Let marinate 6 hours to overnight. Grill over hot coals 40 minutes or until cooked through.

Chicken Cacciatore

To serve four

1 chicken , cut in serving pieces
2–3 Tbl. flour
salt and pepper
¼ c. olive oil
1 onion, chopped
4 cloves garlic, chopped
1 bay leaf
big pinch thyme and marjoram
1 tsp. basil
¼ c. tomato paste
½ c. dry white wine
1 tsp. salt
½ tsp. pepper
¾ c. chicken stock
½ lb. mushrooms, quartered

Season chicken pieces with salt and pepper and dredge in flour. Heat olive oil in heavy sauté pan and brown chicken pieces. Remove from pan and sauté onion until soft and golden brown. Add garlic and herbs and sauté a few minutes more. Add tomato paste, chicken stock, salt, pepper and mushrooms and bring to a boil. Add chicken pieces to pan and simmer, covered, 1 hour or until chicken is tender. Serve with pasta or polenta.

Poulet au Diable
(Devilled Chicken)

To serve four

1 chicken, cut in serving pieces
salt, pepper
4 Tbl. unsalted butter, melted
½ c. mustard, hot Dijon style
½ c. finely chopped green onions
4 cloves garlic, crushed and chopped
2 c. fresh bread crumbs

Season pieces of chicken with salt and pepper and brush with some of the melted butter. Place on broiler pan and under broiler, 10 minutes on each side or until almost done—juices should be almost clear. Remove from oven and drain off and save pan drippings. In a small bowl combine the mustard, green onions and garlic. Beat in the pan drippings. Smear this mixture all over the pieces of chicken, then roll them in the bread crumbs. Return chicken to broiler pan, drizzle with remaining melted butter and return to 375° oven a few minutes until chicken is golden brown and sizzling.

Roast Chicken
with Forty Cloves of Garlic

If forty cloves of garlic sound wild, wait until you start sealing your roasting pan with flour paste—it's one of the whackiest things I've done in the kitchen. And it makes a mess when you crack it open. But it's so much fun to eat your dinner with a hammer, and the smell when you take off the lid is heavenly. The garlic cloves are soft and mellow, and the chicken is so juicy and delicious, it's worth the fuss. P.S— my mother makes this with a Romertopf clay pot: no paste, no mess, no fun.

1 chicken, a fryer to serve 4
   or a roaster to serve 6
salt, pepper
1-2 tsp. rosemary
40 cloves of garlic, more if desired
(the garlic in this dish is truly tamed;
everyone will be clamoring for more)
2–3 c. flour

Sprinkle the chicken inside and out with salt, pepper and rosemary. Peel the cloves of garlic without crushing them. The easiest way to do this is to drop them into a pan of boiling water for 30 seconds. Drain, run under a little cold water to cool them for handling, and the skins will slip right off. Place chicken in a roasting or other pan with a lid—it should fit comfortably without too much space around it. Strew the garlic all around the chicken and put on lid. Make a paste by stirring water into the flour—equal parts of flour and water are about right to make a thick paste that will stay put. Start smearing the paste around the edge of the lid of the pot. Put on a thick layer—you want the pot to be as airtight as possible. When well sealed place pot in a 425° oven. After 15 minutes reduce heat to 375° and bake until chicken is done, 45 minutes for a 3 pound fryer, 1 hour and 15 minutes for a 7 pound roaster. When ready to serve tap the paste, which by now has hardened like plaster, with a hammer. Paste will come off easily in big pieces, so it is possible to do this at the serving table, which makes for great drama. Lift the lid off carefully, so as not to be burned by the steam and take a moment to enjoy the rich aroma. Cut the chicken in serving pieces and serve with the pan juices and the garlic, which may be eaten with the chicken or spread on bread or potatoes. Note: the skin on this chicken does not get brown and crispy, making this a good occasion to be virtuous, and not eat the skin of your chicken!

Fennel Chicken

To serve four

4 oz. pancetta, sliced ½ inch thick
1 red onion, chopped
1 Tbl. olive oil
1 chicken, cut in serving pieces
2 Tbl. flour
2 c. chicken stock
2 Tbl. fennel seed
4 oz. whole blanched almonds
salt and pepper to taste

Cut pancetta in ¼" x 1" strips and sauté with onion in the olive oil. When onion and pancetta are brown remove them and brown chicken in the same pan. When chicken is well browned sprinkle on the flour and cook 2 minutes. Add the chicken stock, fennel, onions, pancetta, almonds, salt and pepper, stir to mix all ingredients and simmer 30 minutes, covered. Skim fat before serving.

David and Wendy, 1953

Herman's Lemon Chicken

This is the first dish my husband made for me when we were courting. I've tried making it at the Ranch, but it's never as good. He hovers over it, basting and turning it constantly, which you just can't do when you have 60 pieces of chicken on a huge grill that singes your eyebrows when you bend over it. And then, of course, there's the love factor; when someone cooks for you with as much love as he does, it's bound to taste good. And, finally, there's the perfection through practice phenomenon. He has a limited number of dishes that he's made thousands of times— this chicken, French toast, onions and eggs, even his hamburgers are the best I've ever tasted.

To serve four

1 chicken, cut in pieces

2 lemons

6–8 cloves of garlic (*I first typed 68 which is probably closer to the number Herman really uses*)

2 Tbl. oil

salt, pepper, paprika

Squeeze the juice of one half lemon over the pieces of chicken. Purée the garlic with the oil in blender. Smear over the chicken, then sprinkle on salt, pepper, and liberal amounts of paprika on both sides. Put chicken on the grill, cover (if using Weber-type grill) and let cook 10 minutes. Turn, squeeze another half lemon over chicken. Continue cooking, turning and squeezing lemon juice over chicken until it is cooked through and skin is dark brown and crisp.

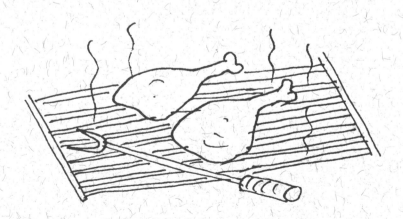

Lemon Ginger Chicken

To serve four

1 chicken, cut in pieces
2 Tbl. oil
1 onion, chopped
2 c. chicken broth
⅓ c. shredded ginger
⅓ c. lemon peel,
    cut in very thin strips
2 Tbl. cornstarch
¼ c. lemon juice
¼ c. soy sauce
salt and pepper

Brown chicken in oil. Remove from pan and sauté onion until soft. Drain off as much oil as possible and return chicken to pan along with lemon peel; add ginger to pan. Add chicken stock, bring to a boil, reduce heat to simmer and cook, covered, for 45 minutes or until chicken is done. Dissolve cornstarch in a small bowl with lemon juice and soy sauce. Stir into chicken and cook 2 minutes. Season to taste with salt and pepper.

Lemon Rosemary Chicken

To serve four

1 chicken, cut in serving pieces
zest and juice of 2 lemons
4 cloves garlic, chopped
2 tsp. rosemary
salt and pepper
1 c. water or ½ c. water
    and ½ c. white wine
4 Tbl. unsalted butter, optional

Lay chicken pieces on a baking pan and sprinkle with the lemon zest, the juice of one lemon, garlic, rosemary, salt and pepper. Place in a 425° oven. Turn chicken pieces and baste with additional lemon juice every ten minutes. When chicken is done, in about 30-40 minutes, remove chicken pieces from pan and keep them warm while preparing sauce. Pour off grease from baking pan and place pan over flame on stovetop. Add water, or water and wine, and bring to a boil, scraping up juices and bits of chicken stuck to pan. Let liquid boil down to about half its volume. Taste and add salt and pepper as needed. As is, this makes a healthful, light "jus" type sauce to spoon over chicken and potatoes or rice. If a richer sauce is desired you may whisk in butter, off the heat, just before serving.

Hoisin Chicken with Cashews

To serve four

1 lb. boneless, skinless
   chicken breast
3 Tbl. tamari or soy sauce
3 Tbl. rice wine or sherry
2 Tbl. chopped ginger
4 cloves garlic, chopped
2 Tbl. oil
½ c. chopped onion
½ lb. mushrooms, slices
1 red bell pepper, cut in strips
½ lb. snow peas, stemmed
½ c. cashews, toasted
¼ c. Hoisin sauce,
   (I prefer Koon Chun brand)
4 Tbl. chopped cilantro, optional

Cut chicken into 1 inch cubes and let marinade one hour or more with tamari, rice wine or sherry, ginger and garlic. To cook heat 1 Tbl. oil in sauté pan and add chicken when oil is hot. Toss and stir constantly until chicken is just cooked. Remove from pan, add 1 Tbl. oil and sauté onion and pepper a few minutes. Add mushroom, and stir fry until vegetables are tender but still crisp. Add snow peas, and stir fry just until snow peas turn bright green. Push vegetables aside to make a well in center of pan and add hoisin sauce. Let heat a few moments, then add chicken and cashews and toss and heat all. Garnish with optional cilantro and serve immediately.

Buttermilk Rosemary Oven Fried Chicken

This dish is too time consuming to prepare for large groups, so whenever we have a small group of only 10 or so I try to make it—it's a staff favorite.

To serve four

1 chicken, cut in serving pieces
1 ½ c. buttermilk, approx.
1 c. flour
2 Tbl. rosemary
1 tsp. each salt and pepper
1 c. oil

Put chicken pieces in a bowl and pour buttermilk over them to cover. Let marinate 1 hour or more. Mix together flour, rosemary, salt and pepper. Lift chicken pieces out of buttermilk one at a time, let the excess buttermilk drain off and dredge chicken in flour. Brown chicken in frying pan with oil. Use spatula to loosen pieces when turning—you don't want to lose any of the wonderful crust. As pieces brown remove them to a baking pan large enough to just hold chicken in one layer and at least one inch deep. When all chicken is brown carefully pour buttermilk from marinade around chicken to a depth of ½ inch. Place dish in oven and bake at 350° 45 minutes to one hour, until chicken is cooked. The buttermilk and the juices from the chicken mix to make a delicious gravy, which can be served directly from the pan, or blended to make a more homogeneous sauce.

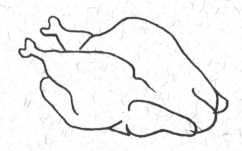

Turkey Chili

This dish came to me from Judy Weiner, one of the best recipe scouts I know. It has an unusual flavor, unlike any other chili I have tasted.

To serve six to eight

½ lb. black beans
1 ½ lb. raw turkey breast, cubed
2 Tbl. olive oil
1 medium onion, chopped
1 ½ Tbl. chili powder
1 ½ Tbl. cumin
1 Tbl. pepper
1 Tbl. cinnamon
3 Tbl. tomato paste
2 tomatoes, diced
2 bottles of beer
4 c. chicken or turkey stock
1 jalapeño, chopped fine
1 small bunch cilantro, chopped
1 tsp. oregano
juice and peel of 1 lemon
salt to taste
Garnishes: sour cream,
            grated cheese,
            chopped green onion
            cilantro

Rinse and soak beans overnight. Cook until soft in chicken stock. Sauté turkey in olive oil with onion. Add seasonings and tomato paste and simmer 5 minutes. Add tomatoes, beer, jalapeño, cilantro, oregano and beans and simmer ½ hour. Salt to taste. Add lemon juice and peel just before serving. Serve with sour cream, grated cheese, chopped green onion and cilantro on the side.

Seafood

Donna Bcullgh '91

THE RANCH BELL

by Wendy Westerbeke

The Bell at the Westerbeke Ranch is a sound full of anticipation and joy for our guests, as well as for those of us who live and work here. Walking through the lush gardens, under the old oak trees, the approach to the Adobe dining room is permeated by the delicious smell of cooking garlic, herbs and homemade bread. As I open the large barn-red doors, pushing firmly on the wrought iron handle, I am greeted by a collage of smells and colors. Long redwood tables, lit by candles and decorated with fresh garden flowers, are set and waiting. A welcoming fire glows in the fieldstone hearth. Colorful Mexican serapes, pottery and Haitian metal work, collected over the years by my family, dot the walls. Rustic fence posts, some still covered with lichen, create the ceiling of this beautiful dining room. Built by my grandparents, this room holds many childhood memories for me, including the time, as an artistic five-year-old, I decorated the walls with bright red nail polish!

As our family ranch became open to the public, many aspects of our buildings and facilities have been developed and enhanced, but the dining room remains virtually the same. Warm, inviting and imbued with a generosity of spirit, the Adobe and adjoining patio are the heart of the Westerbeke Ranch. Guests gather here to feed their bodies and also to feed their souls; meeting new friends, sharing meals together and opening up to the nurturing spirit of the Ranch.

And nurturing it is. Carol and her kitchen staff are part of the innermost heartbeat here. The meals are consistently delightful and delicious, served in a gracious and helpful manner, which is all the more miraculous due to the hectic and demanding cooking schedule under which the staff works year-round.

As the kitchen doors swing open, the buffet is filled with wonderful platters of food, the candles on the hearth are lit, and a little Mozart plays in the background, I know our guests are in for a special treat. And when that meal bell rings again, it will be music to our ears.

Spicy Thai Marinade for Fish

To serve three to four

¼ c. lime juice
1 small bunch cilantro
2–4 cloves garlic
1 fresh jalapeño chile
1" piece of ginger,
    peeled and cut in fourths
2 Tbl. olive oil
½ tsp. salt or to taste

Place all ingredients in blender or food processor and puree. Taste and adjust seasoning. Lime juice may be increased if a tart sauce is desired, more oil and a touch of salt if less tartness is preferred. Jalapeño may be increased or left out. Spoon a small amount over fish filets or steaks and marinate 1 hour before cooking. Bake, broil or grill fish and serve remaining sauce with fish. Makes enough sauce and marinade for 1 ½ lb. fish.

Baked Fish
with Mushroom Sauce

To serve four to five

1 ½ lb. fish filets,
    red snapper, ling cod, etc.
salt, pepper, dill
1 c. dry white wine
4 Tbl. unsalted butter, in all
½ lb. mushrooms, sliced
4 shallots, finely chopped
2 Tbl. flour
¼ c. heavy cream
Lemon juice as needed
Sliced lemon and parsley
    for garnish

Lay fish filets in a buttered baking dish. Sprinkle with salt, pepper, and dill. Dot with 2 Tbl. of the butter and pour wine over all. Cover with aluminum foil or waxed paper and bake at 375° 10-15 minutes or till just cooked through. While fish is cooking start sautéeing the mushrooms. Put 2 Tbl. of the butter and 1 Tbl. oil in sauté pan over high heat. When butter is melted and bubbling add mushrooms and shallots. Stir and toss mushrooms and cook quickly till starting to brown. Add flour and stir into mushrooms. Continue cooking and stirring 2 more minutes. Remove mushroom pan from heat. When fish is cooked remove from oven and carefully pour liquid from fish over the mushrooms. Put mushrooms back on high heat and cook, stirring and scraping bottom of pan. Let mixture simmer and cook down till sauce is thickened and "raw" taste of the wine is gone. Add cream and salt, pepper and lemon juice as necessary. Remove fish from oven, garnish with parsley and sliced lemon, and serve with sauce.

Portuguese Baked Fish

To serve four

1 ½ lb. fish filets, red snapper,
    ling cod or other

1 onion, thinly sliced

2 tomatoes, sliced

¼ lb. mushrooms, sliced

¼ lb. sliced ham, optional

1 Tbl. fresh dill, 1 tsp. dried dill,
    or 2 Tbl. fresh basil, chopped

1 c. dry white wine

2 egg yolks

8–12 Tbl. unsalted butter, softened

Place fish filets flat in a greased baking pan, preferably an attractive one from which the fish may be served at the table. Season with salt and pepper. Lay over the filets the optional ham, onions, tomatoes, and mushrooms. Pour white wine over all and cover dish with buttered aluminum foil or waxed paper. Bake at 375° 15–20 minutes or until fish is just cooked, flaking and no longer translucent. Holding a lid over the pan, carefully pour liquid into a non-aluminum saucepan. Turn off oven and put fish back in to stay warm.

Put saucepan over high heat to boil down liquid. When reduced to ¼ c. remove from heat and beat in egg yolks with a wire whisk. Put pan over low heat and cook gently, whisking continuously, till mixture thickens slightly and becomes foamy, as in making Hollandaise sauce. Off the heat start whisking in butter by the tablespoonful. Add butter till sauce is of the desired thickness (the more butter you add the thicker the sauce gets). Taste for seasoning, adding the herbs as well as salt, pepper or lemon juice as needed. Remove fish from oven and serve with sauce on the side.

Lemon Teriyaki Shark

To serve six

1 small can
    frozen lemonade concentrate
¼ c. soy sauce
4 cloves garlic, chopped
2 Tbl. shredded ginger
2 Tbl. oil
2 lb. shark steaks, or other
    grillable fish (swordfish, tuna,etc.)

Combine all ingredients and pour over shark steaks in a glass or stainless steel dish. Let marinate 2–3 hours, then grill fish over hot coals, about 5 minutes on a side.

Marilyn Goode and Joyce Moulton, Patty's sisters, 1937

Stuffed Filet of Sole

To serve four

1 ¼ lb. Petrale sole filets

2 shallots, finely chopped

¼ lb. mushrooms, finely chopped

4 Tbl. unsalted butter

1 c. fresh bread crumbs
  (*i.e. dried bread ground up
  in blender, not bread-crumbs
  from a bag that taste like sawdust*)

2–4 Tbl. sour cream

1 tsp. tarragon

½ tsp. salt

½ tsp. white pepper

1 Tbl. butter

½ c. white wine

½ c. heavy cream

1 large tomato, peeled, seeded
  and chopped, optional

Sauté shallot and mushroom in butter until soft and mushroom has released its juice. Remove from heat, stir in bread crumbs, salt, pepper and tarragon. Add sour cream if necessary to make a soft, moist stuffing that will hold its shape. Lay out a filet. Mold about ¼ cup of the stuffing into a cylinder the same length as the width of the filet, place it at one end of the filet and carefully roll up the filet enclosing the stuffing. Repeat with rest of filets. Choose a baking pan that will just hold the filets in one layer and butter the bottom. Lay the filets in the dish with the end of the roll facing down. Pour the wine and cream over the fish and cover with lid or buttered wax paper. Bake in a 400° oven till just cooked, about 10 minutes. Remove filets to a plate and keep warm in the turned-off oven. Boil down liquid in dish with the optional tomato until reduced to a sauce consistency, about 5–10 minutes. Season with salt and pepper if needed. To serve spoon a little sauce over each filet and top with a sprig of parsley.

Beurre Blanc

Wine and butter sauce for fish or vegetables

To make one cup

½ c white wine
2 Tbl. finely chopped shallot
1 c softened butter
salt, white pepper
optional: ½ c cream
       1 Tbl. mustard

Bring white wine and shallots to a boil in a stainless steel saucepan (aluminum pan will turn sauce green). Reduce to 2 Tbl. Remove from heat and stir in butter by the tablespoonful. Season with salt and pepper. Add optional cream and mustard if desired.

Beurre Nantais

Make Beurre Blanc (no cream). At the end add:
2 tsp. fresh tarragon
1 Tbl. fresh chervil
2 Tbl. parsley
2 tsp. lemon juice

Hollandaise Sauce

To make one cup

3 egg yolks
½ lb. unsalted butter
2 Tbl. water
1–2 Tbl. lemon juice
½ tsp salt, white pepper
pinch of cayenne pepper

Set butter to melt over a double boiler. When it is melted skim off white foam on top and set butter in a warm place. Put egg yolks and water in a small heavy bottomed saucepan. Start whisking the eggs and place over a very low flame. Gently warm the eggs, stirring constantly. As they begin to warm up they will expand and become very foamy and light. At no time should the sides of the saucepan feel more than very warm to the hand—it should never become too hot to touch. Judging when the eggs are cooked enough is the tricky part. Remove the pan from the heat whenever you have any doubts—just continue whisking as you observe the texture of the eggs. You can always put it back on the stove if you decide it's not cooked enough, but there's nothing to be done with curdled egg yolks, which can happen in a flash. Egg yolks are cooked enough when they thicken slightly and the bottom of the pan can be seen when the whisk is drawn accross it. Immediately remove pan from heat and start pouring in clarified butter in a thin stream. Beat slowly but constantly. Sauce will continue to thicken and fluff up. Season sauce with salt, pepper and lemon juice to taste.

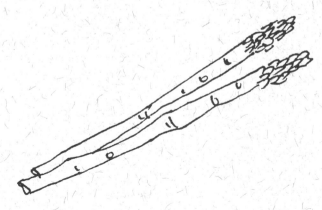

Scallops
in Bacon and Cognac Sauce

Another creation of Cathy Connorton, my catering partner in New York and now head of Chefs a l'Orange in Orange, Connecticut. It is a lovely entree with rice or new potatoes, or may be served on tiny skewers as an hors d'oeuvre.

To serve four

¼ lb. bacon
1 ½ lb. scallops
4 Tbl. unsalted butter
1 shallot, finely chopped
¼ c. cognac or very good brandy
1 c. cream
squeeze of lemon juice
salt and pepper

Cut bacon slices in ½ inch strips and fry until crisp. Drain and set aside. Sauté shallot in butter until soft then add scallops. Cook until scallops have just turned opaque, then add cognac and reduce it rapidly (you may ignite it if you're feeling dramatic. Just be sure to let all the alcohol boil off after the flames go out.) Remove scallops, leaving liquid in pan. Add cream and boil down rapidly to make sauce. Add scallops and bacon and stir a few moments to reheat everything. Season with a little lemon juice, salt and pepper and serve immediately.

Greek Shrimp in Tomato and Feta Cheese Sauce

To serve four

1 ½ lb. medium shrimp, shelled
1/4 c. olive oil
1 onion, chopped
1 tsp. oregano
½ c. white wine
2 c. chopped tomato, fresh or canned
½ c. chopped parsley
½ c. crumbled feta cheese

Sauté onion in olive oil until soft. Add oregano, white wine and tomato and simmer gently 20 minutes. Add shrimp and stir and cook until shrimp turn pink, about 5 minutes. Just before serving stir in feta cheese and parsley. Taste for salt after adding feta—it is very salty. Serve on rice or pasta.

Circa 1938

123

White Sauce (Cream Sauce or Bechamel)

The amount of butter and flour used in this recipe depends on the way it will be used. For a souffle or to mix with the vegetables in the omelette souffle roll (pg. 14) the larger amounts would be used. For a sauce to lighly coat vegetables, for example, the smaller amount would do.

To make one cup

2–4 Tbl. unsalted butter
2–4 Tbl. flour
1 c. milk, scalded
½ tsp. salt, white pepper
optional additions: 1 tsp. mustard,
    1–2 cloves garlic, crushed

Melt the butter in a heavy bottomed saucepan over medium heat. When it is bubbling remove pan from heat and whisk in the flour and optional garlic. Return to heat and cook the roux 2 minutes, stirring constantly. Do not let the flour brown. Again off the heat, whisk in the scalded milk. Return to fire, stirring constantly and let the sauce boil gently 2 minutes. Season with salt, pepper, and optional mustard and garlic.

• **Cheese Sauce:** When sauce is complete stir in 1 c. grated cheese. Cheddar, swiss, and seasoned jack cheeses are all good.

Seafood in Cream Sauce

To serve six

1 lb. fish filets, snapper,
 cod or other
1 lb. scallops
½ lb. prawns
1 c. dry white wine
1 c. water
handful of parsley
1 carrot sliced
1 stalk of celery, sliced
salt, white pepper
6 T. unsalted butter, in all
½ lb. mushrooms, sliced
juice of one lemon
4 T. flour
1 c. hot milk
½ c. heavy cream

Place fish filets in a non-aluminum saucepan. Sprinkle with salt and pepper and strew with parsley, carrots, and celery. Pour wine and water over all. Cover with buttered aluminum foil or waxed paper, place over medium heat and simmer 10 minutes or until just cooked through. Carefully remove fish and add scallops. Simmer them until just cooked and no longer translucent, about 5 minutes. Remove scallops and cook prawns in the same liquid, 5-8 minutes, depening on size. Shell and devein prawns and set aside with fish and scallops. Strain cooking liquid and return to saucepan. Place over high heat and boil down till reduced to 1 c. liquid.

Melt 4 T. butter in saucepan. When butter is bubbling add mushrooms and sauté 5 minutes. Remove pan from heat and whisk in flour. Return to heat and cook 2 minutes, stirring constantly. Do not let flour brown. Pour in reduced cooking liquid and milk. Bring mixture to a boil, stirring constantly. Cook 2-3 minutes, add heavy cream and boil another minute. Taste for seasoning, adding salt, pepper, and lemon juice as needed. Just before serving bring sauce to a boil and fold in fish, scallops and prawns.

Serve over pasta, rice or polenta.

My Dad's Oyster Stew

A father of the fifties, mine never cooked, except for oyster stew. Because it was such an awesome sight to see my dad at the stove, I always revered this dish as extraordinary.

To serve two

10 oz. jar of oysters
4 Tbl. butter
pepper to taste
a few drops Angostura bitters
dash of sugar (optional)
milk as desired

Place oysters with their liquor in a sauce pan with butter and pepper. Add angostura bitters and sugar and bring to a boil. Boil 5 minutes and add milk. Simmer to heat, but do not let stew boil after milk has been added.

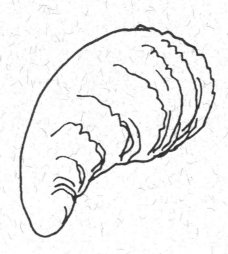

Vegetables

The Most Flavor-Preserving Way
to Cook Vegetables

Although it goes against the grain of the steamed vegetable school, it turns out that vegetables cook the quickest, with the best flavor and color, when boiled in a large quantity of boiling, salted water, as for cooking pasta. Broccoli, green beans, asparagus, peas and spinach in particular are most beautiful and delicious when cooked this way. If you hate to lose contact with any vitamins that may leach into the water, save it and use it for soup. I have no scientific evidence, but I suspect that the shortened cooking time lessens the amount of nutrients lost. In any case, for us, cooking in such large volumes, it is the only practical method. For eating cold or to prepare vegetables ahead of time and then reheat them just before serving at a later time, remove the vegetables from the boiling water and immediately plunge into ice water. This stops the cooking and preserves the wonderful crunch and color.

Bring a large pot of water to a boil, 1 gallon for 1–2 pounds of vegetable. Add 2 tsp. salt. While heating water prepare vegetable for cooking—e.g broccoli cut into flowerettes, green beans snapped and strung, carrots peeled and cut into rounds or sticks, spinach washed in a large quantity of water, asparagus stems peeled and woody ends snapped off, etc. When water is at a full rolling boil drop in vegetables. Start tasting after a few minutes and taste frequently to cook vegetable no more than necessary. Everyone has his or her own standard of doneness; experiment with the different stages in the raw to mushy continuum to discover your own. There are discoveries to be made—I have seen people taste brussel sprouts for the first time since childhood and enjoy them. A little butter, lemon juice and parmesan cheese helps of course, but proper cooking is the foundation.

Soy Garlic Lemon Butter for Vegetables

For 1 lb. vegetable:
4 Tbl. unsalted butter
1 Tbl. tamari (soy sauce)
1 Tbl. lemon juice
1 clove garlic, finely chopped

Melt butter in a small pan. Saute garlic a few minutes over gentle heat—it should not brown. Stir in tamari and lemon juice, taste and adjust seasoning. Pour over steamed vegetables; with green vegetables such as broccoli add butter just before serving—after a few minutes the lemon juice causes the bright green color to turn an unappetizing brownish green.

Ratatouille

Ratatouille is the answer to a gardener's prayers—a delicious way to use those vegetables that start producing with such abandon at the peak of summer, especially zucchini. The name is French but I like to serve it with Italian dishes, especially pesto.

To serve one person per half pound of vegetable

More or less equal quantities, (depending on preference and garden yield), of:
  onion, sliced or chopped
  eggplant, cut in 1" cubes
  zucchini, cut in ½" rounds
  peppers, green or red, cut in strips
  tomatoes, roughly chopped
As much garlic
  as your audience will bear
olive oil
salt, pepper, lots of fresh basil

Sauté each of the vegetables except tomatoes in olive oil until almost done. Keep them separate for this initial cooking as they each need a different length of time to cook. When they are all sauteed combine them with the garlic in a big pot. Give the garlic a few minutes to sauté, then add the tomatoes. Bring all to a simmer and cook gently ½ hour to blend the flavors. Add salt and pepper to taste and fresh chopped basil just before serving. Ratatouille, like any other stew, tastes great the next day and even the next. It also freezes. It can be a side dish or a main dish, especially with a hearty pasta to accompany it. It's good on pizza, in lasagna, and can even be pureed and eaten as soup (see pg. 46).

Tomato Pesto Tart

To serve four

8" pastry shell, partially baked
8 small tomatoes
1 ½ c. ricotta cheese
¼ c. sour cream
¼ c. chopped parsley
1 egg plus 1 egg yolk
1 tsp. each basil, salt, pepper
1 c. pesto sauce

Cut tomatoes in half, scoop out seeds, season with salt and pepper and bake on a lightly oiled baking sheet at 325° 20 minutes. Remove to a wire rack and drain, cut surface down, 20 minutes. Combine remaining ingredients, except for pesto, and pour into pastry shell. Smooth top with a spatula. Place tomatoes on top of ricotta mixture, hollow side up. Bake at 350° 30 minutes or until filling is set. Serve warm or at room temperature. Just before serving fill each tomato with a tablespoonful of pesto sauce.

Tart may also be made with cherry tomatoes and cut in small squares (one tomato to a square) to serve as an hors d'oeuvre. Cut just the tops off cherry tomatoes, scoop out center with a small spoon and bake 15 minutes.

Patty and Don Westerbeke, 1949

Mom's Squash Casserole

If I gave my mother full credit for everything she contributed to this cookbook I would have to retitle it "Marjorie's Cooking". Learning to cook at an early age, learning that cooking is fun and endlessly varied, and learning to give in such a wholesome way is a gift I will never stop treasuring. Cooking with my mother is such a special memory for me; I love continuing the tradition with my sons.

1 medium onion, chopped
½ green pepper, chopped
1 small jalapeño pepper, chopped
2 Tbl. butter
3 eggs
½ lb. monterrey jack cheese, grated
salt and pepper to taste
½ tsp. each, marjoram and oregano
2 large zucchini, sliced
5 small yellow squash, sliced
4 Tbl. butter

Sauté onion, green pepper and jalapeño in 2 Tbl. butter until soft. Put in mixing bowl with eggs, cheese, salt, pepper, and herbs. Sauté zucchini squash briefly in 4 Tbl. butter; don't cook it until it's done or casserole will be mushy. Add vegetables to mixing bowl and pour into a buttered casserole and bake at 350° about 30 minutes, or until golden and set.

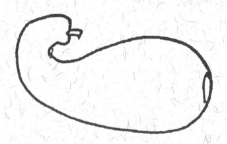

Stuffed Peppers Genovese Style

This hearty, sweet/sour/salty stuffing would be good in other vegetables too, even in a chicken.

To serve eight

8 bell peppers, red preferred
4 c. cooked rice
¼ lb. chopped ham, optional
½ c. capers
½ c. black olives, chopped
½ c. raisins or currants
½ c. chopped onion
1 c. chopped tomato, fresh or canned
½ c. red wine vinegar
½ c. olive oil
salt and pepper to taste

Cut out stems from peppers and shake out seeds. Blanch in a big pot of boiling water about 10 minutes—they should be tender but still hold their shape. Combine remaining ingredients and adjust seasoning. Stuff peppers and place in a baking dish with ¼ " water. Bake at 350° 20–30 minutes or until hot throughout.

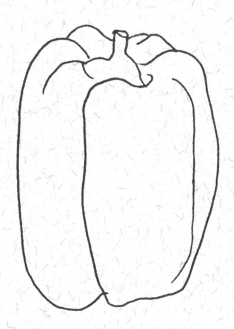

Potatoes au Gratin with Ham

To serve six to eight

3 ½ lb. boiling potatoes

4 Tbl. unsalted butter

⅓ c. flour

1 large clove garlic, chopped fine

2 ¼ c. scalded milk

salt and pepper

nutmeg

1 ½ Tbl. Dijon mustard

2 c. grated cheese, Gruyere, Swiss
  or cheddar (or a mixture)

2–2 ½ c. Smoked ham, sliced
  and cut in strips

Scrub potatoes and cut in ¼" slices. Boil in 2 c. salted water 4 minutes or until just tender. Drain off water and leave covered in pan. Make garlic mustard bechamel: melt butter in saucepan, remove from heat and whisk in flour and garlic. Return to heat and cook 2 minutes, stirring constantly with whisk, taking care not to let roux brown. Off the heat add hot milk and whisk until smooth. Return to heat, boil 2 minutes. Season with salt, pepper, a few gratings of nutmeg and the mustard. Leave slightly undersalted as the cheese and ham will both add saltiness. Spread a small amount of sauce in bottom of baking dish. Spread out ⅓ of potatoes, then ⅓ of sauce, ½ the ham and ⅓ of the cheese. Top with another ⅓ potatoes, ⅓ of sauce, remaining ham and ⅓ cheese. Finish with the rest of the potatoes, sauce and cheese. Bake at 375° 45 minutes or until casserole is bubbling and cheese is golden brown.

Sweet Potatoes with Tangerines and Pecans

To serve four

1 lb. sweet potatoes or yams
2–4 Tbl. unsalted butter
2 tangerines
¼ c. pecans, toasted and chopped
salt and white pepper to taste

Bake sweet potatoes until soft. Cut in half and scoop out flesh. Place in a bowl and mash with butter. Peel tangerine and section. Cut each section in half and remove seeds. Stir into sweet potatoes with pecans and season with salt and pepper. Serve immediately or put in a buttered baking dish and refrigerate. Bake at 350° 20–30 minutes to reheat.

Gado Gado

Gado gado is an Indonesian name for a sauce found in many Asian cuisines, especially Thai. When we tell people it's a spicy peanut butter sauce they often make a face and put the tiniest dab on the edge of their plates. Moments later, however, they come back for more. More than almost any other dish, this seems to capture the rapture of the sweet/sour/ spicy/salty combination of flavors.

To serve four to eight

1 c. chopped onion

2 Tbl. butter or oil

3 cloves chopped garlic

1 c. natural peanut butter

2 Tbl. honey, more to taste

¼ tsp. cayenne, more to taste

2 Tbl. cider vinegar

1 Tbl. chopped fresh ginger

2–3 c. water

1 Tbl. tamari or soy sauce

Sauté onion in butter or oil until soft, about 5 minutes. Add garlic and ginger and sauté 2 minutes longer. Add remaining ingredients, mashing peanut butter with wooden spoon or whisk to mix with water. Add only enough water to make a smooth sauce thin enough for dipping. Let simmer 30 minutes, stirring occasionally. Taste and adjust seasoning.

Serve with raw (carrot and celery sticks, strips of bell pepper) and steamed (broccoli, cauliflower, snow peas, green beans) vegetables and tofu chunks sautéed with mushrooms and bean sprouts.

Hummus

To serve six to eight

1 can garbanzos (chickpeas)
    or 1 c. cooked
¼ c. olive oil
2-4 cloves garlic, crushed
1-2 Tbl. tahini
2 Tbl. lemon juice, more if needed
salt and pepper to taste

Start pureeing garbanzos in blender or food processor and add remaining ingredients with machine running. Taste and adjust seasoning. Garbanzos are pretty bland by themselves so don't be afraid to pour on the garlic and lemon juice. Serve with pita bread or raw vegetables.

Spinach and Tofu Curry

To serve four

2 Tbl. chopped fresh ginger
3–6 cloves garlic, peeled
½ fresh hot chili, cut in fourths
¼ c. water
¼ tsp. garam masala or
    1 tsp. curry powder
1 lb. tofu, cut in cubes
6 Tbl. oil
2 lb. fresh spinach,
    washed and chopped
3 Tbl. heavy cream ,optional

Puree ginger, garlic, and chili with water in blender or food processor to make a smooth paste. Heat oil in a large sauté pan with a lid. Add tofu and sauté on high heat until golden brown. Remove tofu from pan and add the seasoning paste and the garam masala or curry powder. Sauté a few minutes then stir in the spinach. Cover and let spinach cook until wilted and tender—about 5 minutes. Remove cover, add tofu and optional cream and heat well. Add salt to taste.

Tahini Tamari Topping
for Rice and Vegetables

Some of the more purist (extreme? enlightened? fanatical?) groups over the years have requested meals using no animal products whatsoever, no wheat, no oils, no sugar, no salt, and, we snarled at first, no taste. But it is always a pleasure to be proved wrong, and the staff has invariably been delighted to discover that eliminating what we're used to just opens the door to new treats. This is one of the more surprising discoveries.

To make one cup of sauce

3 cloves garlic, chopped
1 onion, chopped
¼ c. water
2 Tbl. soy sauce
½ c. raw tahini
1 c. water
¼ c. nutritional yeast
1 Tbl. lemon juice
additional soy sauce as needed

Simmer garlic and onion in soy sauce and water until soft. Add tahini and water and stir to blend. Simmer gently 10 minutes. Add more water if sauce is too thick. Add nutritional yeast, lemon juice and more soy sauce if needed. This makes a good topping for a rice and vegetable casserole—make it fairly thick and spread it over the casserole half way through baking. With the saltiness of the soy sauce and the tang of lemon it works like a cheese sauce to enrich your casserole without the drawbacks of cheese.

Marinade for Tofu

For 1–2 lbs. tofu, to serve four to six

1–2 lbs. tofu, firm–style
½ oz. dried mushrooms
1 c. water
2 tsp. oregano
2 cloves garlic, finely chopped
¼ c. olive oil
½ c. red wine vinegar
½ c. tamari or soy sauce
½ c. red wine
½ tsp. salt
½ tsp. pepper

Drain tofu and lay blocks on a towel. Place another towel on top of them and a plate or cutting board with about 2 lb. weight on top of them. Leave to drain 20 minutes. Simmer the mushrooms in the water 15 minutes. Lift mushrooms out of water with a slotted spoon and strain the liquid through a fine strainer or coffee filter to remove sand. Toast the oregano in a dry frying pan a few minutes. Put mushrooms, strained liquid, oregano and remaining ingredients in a saucepan and simmer 5 minutes. Put the blocks of tofu in a glass or other non-aluminum dish and pour the hot marinade over them. Allow to marinate at least 2 hours, preferably overnight, refrigerated. Tofu can marinate up to two days and marinade can be reused if it is boiled, strained and refrigerated after use.

Marinated tofu may be barbequed, in blocks or cut in chunks and skewered with vegetables, or may be baked or added to a vegetable stir fry.

Vegetarian Loaf

To serve six

1 onion, chopped
2 Tbl. oil
4 oz. (1 ½ c.) mushrooms, chopped
2 cloves garlic, chopped
1 red bell pepper, chopped
1 tsp. each thyme and dill
½ tsp. each sage and tarragon
salt, pepper
1 ½ c. cooked brown rice
1 ½ c. walnuts, finely chopped
½ c. cashews, finely chopped
4 eggs
1 c. ricotta cheese
¾ lb. grated cheese
   (smoked cheese, fontina, gruyere
   and Parmesan are all good,
   alone or in combination)
¼ c. fresh herbs: parsley, oregano,
   basil, chervil

Sauté onion in oil until soft. Add mushrooms, garlic, bell pepper, dried herbs and salt and pepper. Cook until vegetables are soft. Scrape mixture into a bowl and mix in remaining ingredients. Taste and adjust seasoning. Grease a 9" loaf pan, line with foil or waxed paper and grease again. Pour mixture into pan, smooth top and cover with greased paper or foil. Bake at 350° for 1 hour or until firm. Let cool 5–10 minutes in pan, then remove paper from top, turn out and peel off remaining paper or foil. Slice and serve with marinara sauce (pg. 64), or tahini tamari topping (pg. 138).

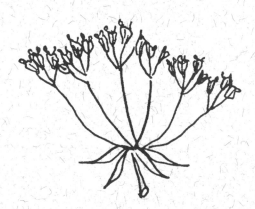

Tomato Sandwich

This is one of those treats you make exactly the way your mother made it for you when you were five years old... The surprise is, it still tastes as good. My catering partner in New York, Cathy Connorton, taught me the ritual. A small bit of perfection. Thanks Betty Anne.

To make one to two sandwiches, depending on size of tomato

1 perfectly ripe garden tomato
    (without the reddest, juiciest
    tomato all else is futile)
2–4 slices Pepperidge Farm
    white bread
1 Tbl. Hellman's mayonnaise
    per sandwich
    (out west it's Best Foods)
salt

Slice tomato ½" thick. Spread each slice of bread with mayonnaise. Lay tomato slices on one piece of bread, sprinkle with salt. Cover with the other slice of bread and let sit 5–10 minutes to allow juices from tomato to mingle with mayonnaise and soak into bread. Eat sandwich over a plate—with the proper tomato you should have a wonderful drippy mess.

Vegetarian Chili

To serve six to eight

4 c. cooked kidney beans

1 c. raw bulgur

2 c. tomato juice

3 Tbl. olive oil

4 cloves garlic, chopped

1 ½ c. chopped onion

1 c. each celery,carrots,
    green pepper, chopped

2 c. tomatoes,
    fresh or canned, chopped

1 Tbl. lemon juice

1 tsp. ground cumin

1 Tbl. chili powder

3 Tbl. tomato paste

3 Tbl. red wine

cayenne, salt to taste

sour cream,
    grated cheese (cheddar or jack),
    and green onions for garnish

Bring tomato juice to a boil and pour over bulgur. Set aside. Saute onions in olive oil for a few minutes and add garlic, celery, carrots, green pepper,and spices. Cook over low heat until vegetables are tender. Add tomatoes, beans, bulgur, lemon juice, tomato paste and red wine and simmer gently 15 minutes. Taste and adjust seasoning. Serve with sour cream, grated cheese, and chopped green onion on the side.

Spanakopita

This Greek spinach pie is one of our favorite lunches—spinach and feta are one of those meant-to-be combinations, and phyllo is unmatched among pastries for its crispness and lightness.

To serve ten to twelve

1 lb. phyllo dough
½ lb. unsalted butter
4 10 oz. pkg. frozen spinach
1 lb. ricotta cheese
½ lb. feta cheese
4 eggs
1 tsp. oregano
½ tsp. salt, or to taste
freshly ground pepper

If phyllo dough is frozen leave in refrigerator overnight to thaw, then leave at room temperature one hour before handling. (Phyllo can be the most maddening stuff in the world to deal with when it starts sticking and tearing, but defrosting in this manner seems to give you the best chance of reasonably cooperative dough.) Set the butter in a double boiler to melt. When it is melted carefully skim off the white foam and spoon the clear butter out of the pan, leaving behind the milky liquids at the bottom. Clarifying the butter thus makes a big difference in the the final crispness of the baked pastry. To make the filling, cook the spinach in a little water briefly to thoroughly defrost it. As soon as it is cool enough to handle (run cold water over it if you are in a hurry), squeeze the spinach a small handful at a time to remove as much water as possible. Place spinach in a bowl and mix with ricotta, feta, eggs, oregano, salt and pepper. Taste and adjust seasonings.

You are now ready to assemble pie. Open the package of phyllo and carefully unroll it. Working quickly so the pastry doesn't dry out, brush the bottom of a 9"x13" pan with butter, and lay one sheet of phyllo in the pan. Brush again with butter and lay on another sheet of pastry. Continue until there are seven layers of pastry. Spread spinach cheese mixture in the pan, then build up another seven layers of phyllo, brushing each layer with the clarified butter. When the last layer is buttered cut through the top half of the pastry with a small sharp paring knife. Diamond shaped pieces are traditional. To make them first cut the pastry lengthwise in fourths, then cut on the diagonal to form diamonds. Place baking sheet in a 400° oven 25-30 minutes or until the pie is puffed, golden brown and set. Remove from oven and cut through the pie all the way. Pie can rest up to fifteen minutes before being served. It may also be frozen and recrisped in oven before serving.

DESSERTS

Do your best   Leave the rest
Angels do no more

My husband taught me this saying and I have it inscribed in my heart and over the door of the kitchen. It's an attitude that is life and spirit-saving in the atmosphere of a kitchen where there are so many things outside of one's control. There will always be last minute changes in menus or guest requests, special diets invented by sadists, extra guests or staff showing up for meals, ingredients you thought were in the pantry just not being there, crucial pieces of equipment conking out at critical moments. When I was green I tried to take responsibility for everything, to account for all those unknowns, or worse yet, to impose enough rules to prevent anything ever going wrong. It made me pretty cranky. It also used to devastate me when someone didn't like my cooking. It would be dishonest to say I no longer care about these things. When I'm tired and frustrated I long for a world where every guest and worker follows every rule, no one ever makes a special request, no one ever brings six extra people to dinner without telling me ahead of time, and everyone always raves about the food. But on the whole I like it better the way it is.

There is very strong feminine energy at the Ranch and in Sonoma, the Valley of the Moon, in general. It is an energy full of beauty, nurturance and creativity, but it is nonlinear, chaotic and overwhelming at first. Invariably, people who start working here soon come up with lists of ways to improve efficiency, eliminate waste and be more "business-like". Some ideas are very good, are readily taken up, and do make life a little easier. As a guiding principle though, efficiency and linear thinking don't seem to take hold. Cynics might say it's because there's a bunch of neurotic women running the place; I suspect that it's more likely the female underneath us all, good old mother earth, who creates a lot of the havoc. Physical evidence of her work is all around—cobwebs woven overnight, little creatures that wander into cabins in the dark, water that streams everywhere in a hard rain, snakes and frogs and worms that swim in the pool, deer that brazenly munch the corn behind the gardener's back. Just as the muck and the slimy critters are underneath every beautiful flowerbed at the Ranch, so too are those darker sides of creativity—chaos and human error—under the tranquil beauty and delicious food that nurtures the souls and stomachs of our guests.

Basic Pastry Dough

Pie dough is one of the most feared undertakings in cooking and with good reason. It requires a balance of confidence in handling with lightness of touch that comes only with years of practice. I'm still not satisfied with my pies. When I achieve the flaky, melt away quality one dreams of, I feel lucky rather than masterful. My mother's pie dough is still my standard of excellence. She has no fancy tricks, just flour, shortening, salt and water, but her pies are heavenly. I even put her to work in the Ranch kitchen when she comes to visit.

The ingredients for pastry are inexpensive enough that it's a worthwhile investment to just make batches to practice handling and rolling out. And the proportions are easy to remember—3 parts flour to one part shortening, the same amount of salt in teaspoons as you have shortening in cups. Water is never measured; the uncertainty of it is part of the mystique.

To make a 2 crust 9" pie or 2 single crust pies

2 c. flour
⅔ tsp. salt
⅔ c. shortening
add water to make a dough

Mix flour and salt in a bowl. Measure shortening, the time honored way being to measure by displacement in a measuring cup of water; for example, put 1 ⅓ c. water in a 2 cup measuring cup and float enough shortening to bring the water line up to 2 cups. The theory is that you thus avoid having to wash a measuring cup covered with shortening, but I usually get some on the cup anyway. I still love to do it—ties to my female ancestors and all that. At any rate, add the shortening to the flour and cut it in with a pastry blender. You can use two knives or your fingers, but since you're going to be making a lot of pastry as you practice to become a master patissier, why not invest in a pastry blender. The shortening should be blended in until there are no more discernable chunks of shortening. "The consistency of coarse cornmeal" is the usual description. At this point start sprinkling on water (cold from the tap is fine) and stirring with a fork. You want to add just enough water to make the pastry hold together. Not enough and the pastry is crumbly and won't hold together when you roll it out, too much and it's sticky and tough. Start out with ⅓ c. water and add more by the teaspoonful until the dough holds together. Form it into a ball with your hands then press it into a flat round about an inch thick. It is ready to be rolled out immediately or can be refrigerated, but be sure and let it warm up 20–30 minutes before attempting to roll it out. Divide dough in two to roll out; for a 2 crust pie make one part a little bigger than the other to be the bottom crust. If pre-baking pie prick abundantly with tines of a fork to keep dough from puffing up out of shape in the oven. A fully pre-baked pie shell will take about 15 minutes in a 400° oven, partially baked about 10 minutes.

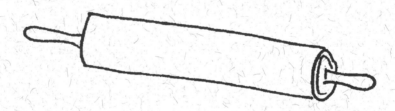

Cream Cheese Pastry

To make 3 dozen small pastries

1 c. butter
8 oz. cream cheese
¼ c. heavy cream
3 c. flour
1 tsp. salt

Cream butter and cream cheese until perfectly smooth and fluffy. Gradually work in cream, then 2 ¾ c. flour. Add up to another ¼ c. flour to make a smooth pliable dough that is no longer sticky.

Refrigerate ½ hour before rolling out. If held longer and dough is very stiff, let it sit out at room temperature until it softens slightly.

Cookie-type Pastry Dough

Unlike most pastry doughs you don't have to worry about over-handling this dough. With so much butter in it you couldn't make it tough if you tried.

For two 9" or eight 4" tart pans

2 c. flour
3 Tbl. sugar
½ tsp. salt
1 c. unsalted butter, cut in pieces
grated zest of one lemon

Mix flour, sugar and salt in an electric mixer or food processor. Add butter and lemon zest and process until dough forms a ball. Press into tart pans and chill 30 minutes. Bake at 375° 12–15 minutes or until golden brown. Let cool before filling. This pastry is especially good with the lemon tart filling.

Lemon Tart

Makes enough filling for 2 9" pastry shells, pre-baked (or save ½ the filling for later use- it will keep in refrigerator for 2-3 weeks).

6 eggs
5 egg yolks
⅓ c. grated lemon rind
2 c. sugar
1 c. lemon juice
½ lb. plus 3 Tbl. soft unsalted butter

Beat thoroughly with wire whisk whole eggs, yolks, sugar, lemon juice and rind. Over a double boiler cook 15 minutes or until thick, stirring constantly. Immediately remove from heat if custard seems to be thickening too fast on the bottom. Beating with whisk off heat should smooth out custard. Let custard cool 15 minutes, stirring frequently. Then beat in the butter, a few tablespoons at a time. Pour custard into pie shells and put under broiler for a few minutes till top is just turning golden brown. Let cool or chill. Garnish with whipped cream to serve.

Patty Van Hoosear, 1938

Harriet's Pecan Pie

My friend Harriet Brown gave me this recipe years ago along with some delicious fresh Texas pecans. She is one of the most creative and fun hostesses I know. I will never forget a July 14th dinner party at her home in Los Angeles when the guests had to storm a paper Bastille to get to the dining room.

To serve eight

1 unbaked 9" pie shell
1 c. sugar
1 c. dark corn syrup
3 Tbl. butter
1 Tbl. flour
3 eggs, beaten
1 tsp. vanilla
pinch of salt
1 Tbl. dark rum
2 c. pecans

Put sugar and dark corn syrup in a small heavy saucepan and slowly heat to a boil. Let simmer 5 minutes. Remove from heat, add butter and let cool 15 minutes. Beat eggs with vanilla, salt and rum and pour into sugar mixture. Beat till thoroughly mixed. Sprinkle pecans evenly in pie crust, then pour syrup over all. Bake at 350° 45-50 minutes or till puffed and set. Knife inserted in center will come out clean. Let cool. Serve with whipped cream or ice cream.

Mystery Pecan Pie

To serve six to eight

Cream cheese layer:
- 8 oz. cream cheese, softened
- ⅓ c. sugar
- ¼ tsp. salt
- 1 tsp. vanilla
- 1 egg

Combine thoroughly and spread in bottom of a 9" unbaked pie shell.

Pecan layer:
- 1 ¼ c. Pecans
- 3 eggs
- ¼ c. sugar
- 1c. dark corn syrup
- 1 tsp. vanilla

Sprinkle pecans over cream cheese mixture. Combine remaining ingredients and carefully pour over pecans. Bake at 375° 25-30 minutes or till puffed and set. Let cool before serving.

Black Bottom Pie

1 9" baked pie shell
1 pkg. gelatin
¼ c. cold water
2 c. milk
½ c. sugar
4 tsp. cornstarch
3 eggs, separated, plus 1 egg yolk
1 ½ oz. unsweetened chocolate,
　　melted or finely chopped
½ tsp. vanilla
1–3 Tbl. dark Meyer's rum
¼ tsp. cream of tartar
¼ c. sugar
1 c. whipping cream
2 Tbl. sugar
½ tsp. vanilla

Soak gelatin in water and set aside. Scald milk in a heavy bottomed saucepan. While it is heating mix well with a whisk in a mixing bowl: ½ c. sugar, cornstarch and 4 egg yolks. Slowly pour hot milk over the mixture and stir well. Pour mixture back into saucepan and return to heat. Cook, stirring constantly over low heat, until custard thickens and coats a spoon heavily. Remove from heat.

Take out 1 cup of custard and mix with the chocolate. Set aside to cool. Add softened gelatin to remaining hot custard. Stir well to be sure gelatin dissolves completely. When custard has cooled somewhat but is not yet stiff, stir in rum to taste. Whip egg whites with cream of tartar till soft peaks form. Add gradually ¼ c. sugar and whip until stiff peaks form. Fold egg whites into rum flavored custard.

Stir ½ tsp. vanilla into chocolate custard and pour into bottom of baked pie shell. Pour rum custard over the chocolate. Chill pie 1 hour or more. Before serving whip cream with 2 Tbl. sugar and ½ tsp. vanilla until stiff. Cover pie with whipped cream, swirling top decoratively. Pie may be garnished by grating or shaving ½ oz. semisweet chocolate over the pie.

Pecan Fudge Pie

To serve eight

Prepare brownie recipe (pg. 177) with only ½ c. flour and 2 c. pecan halves. Pour into a 9" unbaked pie shell and bake at 375° 25–30 minutes or until pie crust is golden and filling is puffed and almost set.

Nut Tart with Chocolate Glaze

To serve ten to twelve

One 11" tart shell, unbaked, chilled
   (use pastry recipe pg.130
   with 1 ½ c. flour)
1 ½ c. sugar
½ c. water
3 ½ c. pecans or walnuts, chopped
1 ¾ c. unsalted butter
⅞ c. milk
⅓ c. honey
8 oz. semisweet chocolate
½ stick unsalted butter
1 tsp. vegetable oil
pinch of salt
20 nut halves for garnish
1 c. heavy cream,
   whipped and sweetened

Boil sugar and water until lightly caramelized. Off the heat add nuts, 1 ¾ c. butter, and milk. Simmer 15 minutes. Off the heat add honey and pour into tart shell. Bake at 425° 20–25 minutes. Let cool. Melt chocolate in a double boiler. Remove from heat and beat in ½ stick butter, oil and salt. Spread over tart. Garnish with nut halves and whipped cream.

Banana Pie

I created this dessert for Dan Millman and his Peaceful Warriors, who like their sweets without sugar, eggs or dairy products. It's also wheat-free. Amazingly, it's also delicious.

To serve six to eight

Crust:

1 c. nuts: almonds, walnuts, pecans
    or a combination of 2 or 3

¼ c. sunflower seeds

¼ c. peanut, cashew or almond butter

¼ c. honey

Filling:

4–5 very ripe bananas

1 tsp. lemon juice

1 tsp. cinnamon

1 tsp. vanilla

1–2 Tbl. honey, optional

Finely grind nuts and sunflower seeds in blender or food processor. Add nut butter and honey and process to blend well. (If using a blender remove ground nuts to a bowl and stir in nut butter and honey.) Press into a 9" pie pan.

Puree or mash bananas. Add lemon juice, cinnamon, and vanilla. Taste and add honey if additional sweetness is required. Pour into pie shell and freeze 2-3 hours or until filling is firm. If frozen very solid let sit at room temperature 15-20 minutes to soften slightly.

Variation: Replace 2 bananas with 2 c. blackberries, raspberries or blueberries, pureed.

Sour Cream Apple Pie

1 9" graham cracker crust, unbaked

Filling:

5–6 medium cooking apples,
   peeled, cored and sliced

1 ½ c. sour cream

2 eggs

1 c. sugar

1 tsp. vanilla

1 tsp. cinnamon

2 Tbl. flour

Topping:

1 c. flour

¾ c. brown sugar

½ c. butter, melted

1 tsp. cinnamon

½ c. chopped walnuts

Spread apples on a lightly buttered baking dish, cover with foil, and bake at 350° 20–30 minutes or until apples are almost tender. Beat eggs a few minutes and stir in sour cream, sugar, vanilla, cinnamon and flour. Scrape baked apple slices into pie shell and pour sour cream mixture over all. Bake another 15–20 minutes or until custard is almost set. Mix topping ingredients together and crumble over pie. Raise oven temperature to 375° and return pie to oven for 10 minutes to brown topping. Let pie cool, and refrigerate before serving.

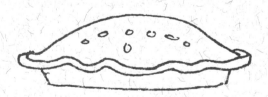

Tarte Tatin—Apple Upside Down Tart

To serve eight

Pastry dough
   made with 1 ¼ cup flour,
   ¼ c. shortening and ¼ c. butter
8 golden delicious apples,
   peeled, cut in half and cored
4 Tbl. unsalted butter
1 c. sugar
1 tsp. cinnamon
¼ c. water

Melt butter in an 8" heavy frying pan—cast iron is ideal. When butter is bubbling add sugar and water. Let heat till sugar is dissolved and forms a bubbling syrup, then cook until syrup is lightly caramelized. With pan still over flame start placing apple halves, standing on end, in pan in an overlapping circle until all fit in.

Sprinkle with cinnamon. Let cook 10–15 minutes until apples start to soften and yield their juices. Roll out pastry in a circle two inches bigger than frying pan. Lay pastry over apples, trimming extra pastry and tucking in edges. Make a few slits in pastry and place in a 375° oven 25–30 minutes or until pastry is puffed and brown. Remove from oven. Place a serving dish at least three inches greater in diameter than the tart pan over frying pan and invert tart. Take great care while flipping pan over that juices do not run down pan and onto exposed skin. Scrape any juices remaining in pan onto tart. Serve warm with vanilla ice cream, whipped cream or créme anglaise.

Strawberry Rhubarb Pie

To serve eight

Pastry for a 2 crust pie
4 c. rhubarb, cut in ½ inch pieces
1 basket strawberries,
   washed, stemmed and sliced
1 ¼ c. sugar
⅓ c. flour

Mix flour and sugar and stir into fruit. Let stand while preparing and rolling out pastry. Fill pie with fruit, cover with pastry and cut several slits in pastry top to let steam escape. Bake at 400° 15 minutes. Reduce heat to 350° and

bake another 40 minutes or until pastry is golden and pie juices are bubbling. Let pie cool at least 30 minutes before serving.

Pear and Almond Tart

To serve eight

Partially baked 9 in. pie shell
1 ¼ c. whole almonds
⅓ c. sugar
2 eggs
⅓ c. heavy cream
¼ tsp. almond extract
1 large or 2 small perfectly ripe pears peeled, cored and roughly chopped

Grind almonds in food processor, blender or grinder till very fine. Mix with remaining ingredients and pour into pie shell. Bake 25-30 minutes at 350° or till filling is puffed slightly and firm in the center. Serve with whipped cream and raspberry sauce.

Note: Most recipes using ground almonds ask you to blanch them first (plunge in boiling water and then slip skins off). I discovered one day when I was in a big hurry that it's not necessary to skin the almonds—the end product is a little darker brown but it tastes just as nice.

The Patio, 1940

Carrot Cake I

To serve twelve to sixteen

1 ½ c. vegetable oil
2 c. sugar
1 tsp. vanilla
1 small can crushed pineapple
2 c. grated carrots
3 eggs
3 c. flour
1 tsp. cinnamon
½ tsp. fresh grated nutmeg
2 tsp. baking soda
1 tsp. salt
1 c. chopped pecans

Combine oil, sugar, vanilla, pineapple, carrots and eggs. Sift together flour, cinnamon, nutmeg, baking soda and salt. Add to carrot mixture. Stir just to mix, then stir in pecans. Pour into three 9" greased and floured cake pans. Bake at 350° 25–30 minutes or until tester comes out clean. Remove cakes from oven, let cool 5 minutes, then turn out on cake racks to cool. Frost with cream cheese frosting (pg. 160).

Carrot Cake II

To serve twelve to sixteen

1 ½ c. oil
2 c. sugar
4 eggs
3 c. grated carrots
1 tsp. vanilla
2 c. flour
2 tsp. cinnamon
2 tsp. baking soda
1 tsp. baking powder
1 tsp. salt
cream cheese frosting, (pg. 160)
2 c. walnuts, chopped

Combine oil, sugar, eggs, carrots, and vanilla. Sift dry ingredients together and stir into carrot mixture. Pour batter into a 9"x13" greased baking pan. Bake at 350° 30–35 minutes. When cool, top with cream cheese frosting to which 2 c. chopped walnuts have been added.

Cream Cheese Frosting

To frost two or three 9" cakes

8 oz. cream cheese, softened

4 oz. (1 stick) unsalted butter,
    softened

½ box (approx 2 ½ c.) powdered sugar,
    sifted

1 tsp. vanilla

2–3 Tbl. milk

Beat cream cheese and butter together until very smooth . Beat in powdered sugar ½ cup at a time, then the vanilla. Add as much milk as necessary to make frosting of spreading consistency.

Fresh Ginger Gingerbread

To serve eight

½ c. unsalted butter, softened

½ c. brown sugar

½ c. molasses

1 egg

½ tsp. salt

1 ½ c. flour

1 tsp. baking soda

½ c. buttermilk

2 oz. fresh ginger, peeled and grated
    (about ¼ c.)

Cream butter, sugar and molasses. Add egg and salt and beat until smooth. Combine flour and baking soda. Add to butter mixture alternately by halves with buttermilk. Stir in ginger. Pour into a greased 8" square pan. Bake at 350° 35–40 minutes. Serve warm or cool with whipped cream.

Wine Cake

This is a very simple white cake that uses oil and white wine instead of butter and milk, making it a good choice for those avoiding dairy products.

To serve sixteen

2 c. sugar
4 eggs
1 c. vegetable oil
1 c. white wine
2 ½ c. flour
½ tsp. salt
2 ¼ tsp. baking powder
1 tsp. vanilla

Beat eggs and sugar in an electric mixer for a few minutes. Add remaining ingredients and beat for one minute. Pour batter into two 9" round or one 9"x13" rectangular cake pans which have been greased and floured. Bake at 350° for 30 minutes or until cakes test done. Let cakes cool 5 minutes before turning out on a rack. Sheet cake may be left in pan. Frost cake with chocolate frosting, or serve with fresh berries and whipped cream.

the Van Hoosear Girls, 1936

Spiced Pecan Cake

To serve sixteen

2 c. pecans, coarsely chopped
¼ c. brown sugar
2 Tbl. cinnamon
1 tsp. nutmeg
¼ c. unsalted butter, softened
2 Tbl. plus 2 tsp. vanilla
¾ c. unsalted butter
2 c. sugar
3 c. flour, sifted
1 tsp. salt
2 Tbl. baking powder
1 c. plus 2 Tbl. milk
3 egg whites

Roast pecans on an ungreased baking sheet at 425° for 10 minutes, stirring occasionally. While they are toasting mix brown sugar, cinnamon, nutmeg, and butter in a 1 qt. bowl. After the ten minutes are up, add the pecans to the bowl and toss to coat them well. Return pecans to oven for 5 minutes. Pour on 2 Tbl. vanilla, stir well and return to oven for 5 more minutes. Remove from oven and set aside to cool. In a mixing bowl beat ¾ c. butter and 1 ½ c. sugar until light and fluffy. Sift flour with salt and baking powder. Add flour mixture and milk to butter/sugar mixture alternately by thirds. Stir in the 2 tsp. vanilla and the pecans. Whip the egg whites until stiff but not dry, then beat in ½ c. sugar. Fold egg whites into the batter. Pour into 3 8" cake pans that have been buttered and floured. Bake at 350° 25–30 minutes or until cake tester inserted into center of cake comes out clean. Let cakes cool in pans 5 minutes then turn them out onto cake racks to cool completely. Frost with Pecan Frosting (next page).

Pecan Frosting

1 ½ c. sugar
¾ c. water
8 egg yolks
¾ c. unsalted butter, softened
¾ c. margarine, softened
2 ½ c. powdered sugar
4 tsp. vanilla
2 ½ c. pecans, toasted and chopped

Bring water and granulated sugar to a boil in a 1 qt. saucepan. Let boil, covered, for 2 minutes to steam down sugar crystals that may have formed on sides of pan. Remove lid and let syrup boil, without stirring, to the soft thread stage (230°), about 15 minutes. Near the end of the cooking time start beating the egg yolks in a mixer on high speed. With mixer running at slow speed pour hot sugar syrup in a thin stream over egg yolks. Do not scrape down drops of syrup that stick to beaters and sides of bowl. Increase speed to high and beat until mixture is cooled, thick and pale. On medium speed add the butter and margarine a few tablespoons at a time. Then add powdered sugar and vanilla and beat until smooth. Stir in pecans and frost cake.

Genoise (Sponge Cake)

An incredibly versatile cake, it's also very simple and quick to make. Of all the recipes I garnered in France this is probably the one I use most—it's just so handy to have around. I have to confess my American tongue is unconverted—the true French sponge has neither salt nor vanilla but it's just too bland for me.

To serve eight

Note: I give these measurements in cups but in French it's much easier—for each large egg you use 30 grams (just over 1 oz.)each of sugar and cake flour. It makes it so simple to make as large or as small a cake as you need.

3 eggs
¼ tsp. salt
1 tsp. vanilla
½ c. sugar
¾ c. cake flour
4 Tbl. melted butter, optional

Beat eggs, salt and sugar a few minutes with a wire whisk or electric mixer, then place mixing bowl over a pan of simmering water and continue beating. The heat helps the eggs expand but too much will cook them. When mixture feels very warm to the touch (104°) remove from heat and continue beating.

The mixture will lighten both in texture and color. Beat until it is cool and "forms the ribbon", that is, when the beater is lifted the batter falls back into to the bowl slowly enough to leave a ribbon of batter on the surface before its falls back into the mass. Beat in vanilla briefly and stir in melted butter if cake is to be used as is, without a flavoring sauce or syrup. Sift the flour over the surface and fold it in quickly but gently by hand. Pour batter into a greased and floured 8" cake pan and bake at 350° 15-20 minutes or until puffed, golden and set.

Things to do with sponge cake

• Brush with a flavoring syrup (4 Tbl. powdered sugar dissolved in 3 Tbl. hot water then mixed with 2 Tbl. liqueur) then fill with fresh fruit and whipped cream.

• Trifle: Cut pieces of cake to fit the bottom of a pretty glass bowl and brush with liqueur flavored syrup (sherry is traditional, I use half sherry and half rum). Cover with sliced sweetened fruit such as raspberries or strawberries, custard sauce and whipped cream.

• Chocolate Mousse Cake: Replace 3 Tbl. of the flour with unsweetened cocoa powder in the cake. Make 2 thin layers of cake. After cakes are baked, removed from the pans and cooled return one layer to the pan and brush with rum flavored syrup. Fill almost to the top with chocolate mousse (pg. 179) and cover with the other layer of sponge cake. Brush it with syrup as well, cover with plastic wrap and refrigerate at least two hours. Serve with whipped cream.

Chocolate Cake

This us my favorite all-American chocolate cake. It's very chocolaty but light and has a beautiful fine crumb.

To serve ten to twelve

4 oz. unsweetened chocolate
½ c. unsalted butter
2 c. brown sugar
3 eggs
1 tsp. vanilla
2 c. flour
2 tsp. baking soda
½ tsp. salt
1 c. sour cream or yogurt
1 c. hot coffee

Melt chocolate over double boiler and set aside to cool. Sift flour, baking soda and salt and set aside. Beat butter and brown sugar in mixer till fluffy. Add eggs one at a time, beating well after each addition. Stir in cooled chocolate and vanilla. Add flour mixture, sour cream and coffee alternately by thirds. Pour batter into buttered and floured or paper-lined cake pans, either 2 9" rounds or one 9"x13" rectangular pan. Bake at 350° 25–30 minutes or until toothpick inserted in center comes out clean. Let cool 5 minutes then turn cakes out onto cake racks to cool (sheet cake may be left in pan). Ice with chocolate frosting or whipped cream.

Chocolate Frosting

This is heady stuff—I mistakenly put it on a child's birthday cake once and the kids couldn't eat it— too rich and not sweet enough. But if you like chocolate strong and straight it's perfect. Just be careful not to overbeat it—it can "seize up" and turn to chocolate butter.

To frost a 2 layer 9" cake:

1 lb. semisweet chocolate
1 c. heavy cream
2 egg yolks

Chop chocolate and melt in a double boiler. Beat cream and egg yolks with an electric mixer a few seconds. Pour in the melted chocolate while it's still warm. Beat for 2 minutes. Let rest 10 minutes, beat again for a few seconds, then frost cake immediately before frosting sets up.

Chocolate Buttermilk Cake

To serve sixteen

1 c. unsalted butter
1 c. water
½ c. cocoa
2 c. sugar
2 c. flour
1 tsp. vanilla
1 tsp. salt
1 tsp. baking soda
½ c. buttermilk
1 tsp. cinnamon, optional

Bring water to a boil with butter and cocoa. When butter is melted and cocoa dissolved add to remaining ingredients and stir well. Pour into a buttered 9"x13" baking pan and bake 20-25 minutes at 450°. While still warm make glaze and spread over cake.

Glaze

¼ c. butter
¼ c. milk
¼ c. cocoa
2 ½ c. confectioners sugar, sifted

Melt butter with milk and cocoa. Stir in sugar.

Note: Cinnamon adds a wonderful note to chocolate.I associate the flavor combination with Mexican food and like to use cinnamon when making a dessert to follow a Mexican meal.

Chocolate Fudge Pudding-Cake

Pudding cakes are so much fun—like 2 desserts in one. And fun to make—it seems impossible that a thick glob with water poured on top could turn into a fudgy cake with a pudding-like sauce on the bottom, but that's exactly what happens.

To serve six to eight

¾ c. flour
⅔ c. sugar
¾ c. unsweetened cocoa
1 ½ tsp. baking powder
½ tsp. salt
½ c. milk or water
4 Tbl. vegetable oil
⅔ c. lightly packed brown sugar
½ c. semisweet chocolate chips
½ c. chopped pecans or walnuts, optional
1 tsp. vanilla
1 ½ c. hot water

Mix together flour, sugar, ½ c. cocoa, baking powder, salt, milk or water and oil. Stir quickly till just blended and spread in an ungreased 8" square baking pan. Mixture will be thicker than usual cake batter. Sprinkle evenly over top brown sugar, ¼ c. cocoa, chocolate chips and optional nuts. Mix vanilla and hot water and carefully pour over all. Bake at 350° 25-30 minutes, until surface looks set and cake like.

Serve warm or cold with ice cream or whipped cream.

Chocolate Cake with Scotch

To serve eight

7 oz. semisweet chocolate,
    chopped in small pieces

3 Tbl. water

½ c. unsalted butter,
    cut in small pieces

3 eggs, separated

⅔ c. sugar

½ tsp. salt

1 tsp. vanilla

¼ c. flour

¼ c. currants or raisins

¼ c. Scotch whiskey or rum

5 oz. (⅔ c.) almonds,
    blanched and finely ground

In a small bowl combine currants (or raisins) and Scotch (or rum) and let soak. Place chocolate, water and butter over a double boiler to melt. When melted stir and set aside to cool. Beat egg yolks, sugar, salt and vanilla at high speed until pale yellow and fluffy. Stir in cooled chocolate/butter mixture, then fold in flour and almonds, then the currants and Scotch. Beat the egg whites with a pinch of salt until stiff but not dry and then fold them into the batter by thirds. Pour batter into a greased and floured 8½"x2" deep cake pan and bake at 375° 20 minutes or until edges are firm but center is still moist. Let cool 5-10 minutes in pan then turn out onto rack to cool. Ice with Chocolate Glaze and serve with whipped cream.

Chocolate Glaze

For each 8"–9" layer of cake:

4 oz. semisweet chocolate, chopped

4 Tbl. unsalted butter

4 Tbl. powdered sugar

Melt chocolate in a double boiler. Stir in butter and sugar a little bit at a time. Beat until smooth and spread immediately on cake.

Photo Galerie Chocolate Cake

This is one of those recipes a friend of a friend obtained and everyone along the line was sworn never to reveal it to another living soul. That was in Paris more than ten years ago—I share it now without fear. The Photo Galerie by the way, was a charming and chic cafe that also, surprise surprise, exhibited photographs.

I have never converted this recipe to American measurements—for me its charm lies in the offbeat way in which it's made.

To serve six to eight

4 eggs
Semisweet chocolate
Unsalted butter
Sugar
2 oz. flour
Pinch of salt
1 tsp. vanilla

Weigh eggs (in shells). Measure out the same weight of chocolate, sugar and butter. Melt chocolate in a double boiler. Off the heat beat in butter by tablespoonfuls until mixture is smooth and thick. Beat eggs, sugar, vanilla and salt in an electric mixer until pale yellow and fluffy. Fold in chocolate butter mixture then flour. Pour batter into a greased and floured loaf pan. Place pan in a bain marie—a larger pan with enough hot water in it to come halfway up the sides of the loaf pan. Bake at 300° 1–1¼ hours, until cake is set but still moist in center—it's half way between a cake and chocolate fudge. Slice from pan and serve with créme anglaise (very French) or whipped cream.

Rocky Road Cake

When I first made this cake for a young friend's twelfth birthday I was filled with remorse and misgivings; her mother would be horrified that I'd tried to poison her family with all that sugar and marshmallows, and everyone would hate it because it would be too sweet and gooey to eat—the icing alone is about an inch thick. To my great surprise they loved it, even Mom. I am learning there's no limit to a kid's appetite for sugar or to a parent's capacity for birthday indulgences. Thank goodness!

To serve sixteen

½ c. butter

½ c. oil

1 c. water

2 c. flour

1 ¾ c. sugar

1 tsp. salt

⅓ c. cocoa

2 eggs

½ c. buttermilk

1 tsp. baking soda

1 ½ tsp. vanilla

Bring butter, oil and water to a boil in a small saucepan. Off the heat stir in cocoa. Set aside to cool. Combine flour, sugar and salt in a mixing bowl. Pour in cocoa mixture and beat just until smooth. Beat in the eggs, then stir in the buttermilk and soda and the vanilla. Batter will be very thin. Pour into a greased 13"x9" baking pan and bake at 350° 30–35 minutes or until cake tests done. Let cool in pan completely before frosting.

Rocky Road Frosting

½ c. cocoa

⅓ c. buttermilk

½ c. butter

3 ½ c. powdered sugar, or enough to make frosting spreadable

⅔ c. miniature marshmallows

½ c. chopped walnuts

1 tsp. vanilla

Melt butter with buttermilk and cocoa in a saucepan over low heat. Remove from heat and beat in enough powdered sugar to make icing of spreadable consistency. Stir in marshmallows, walnuts and vanilla and spread over cake.

Easy Chocolate Cake

I'm sure I could make this cake in my sleep. It can be assembled so quickly and, having no butter or milk, works for many restricted diets.

To serve six to eight

3 oz. unsweetened chocolate
¾ c. water
1 ¼ c. flour
1 c. sugar
½ tsp. baking soda
½ tsp. salt
1 egg
⅓ c. vegetable oil
1 tsp. vanilla
½ c. chocolate chips
½ c. chopped nuts

Melt chocolate with water in a small saucepan. Combine with remaining ingredients, except chocolate chips and nuts, and pour into an 8" greased baking pan. Sprinkle with the chocolate chips and nuts. Bake at 350° 20-25 minutes or until cake tester comes out clean.

Circa 1955

Oatmeal Cookies

To make four to six dozen cookies:

¾ c. unsalted butter

1 c. sugar

2 c. brown sugar

2 eggs

¼ c. water

2 tsp. vanilla

1 ½ c. flour

2 tsp. cinnamon

1 tsp. salt

1 tsp. baking soda

6 c. old fashioned oats

2 c. raisins

optional: 2 c. chopped nuts

2 c. chocolate chips

1 c. coconut

Cream butter and sugars until light and fluffy. Beat in eggs one at a time, beating well after each addition and then add water and vanilla. Sift together flour, cinnamon, salt, and baking soda. Stir flour into batter and mix well. Add oats, raisins and optional ingredients. Place dough by spoonfuls onto greased cookie sheets, leaving 2" space between each cookie. Bake at 350° 10–15 minutes.

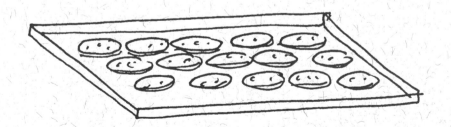

Pecan Bars

To make 36 1 ½"x2" bars

1 c. flour
½ c. unsalted butter
¼ c. brown sugar
3 eggs
1 ¼ c. pecans, chopped
½ c. coconut
1 ¼ c. brown sugar
2 Tbl. flour
½ tsp. salt
1 tsp. vanilla
1 ½ c. powdered sugar
3–4 Tbl. lemon juice

Cut butter into 1 c. flour and ¼ c. brown sugar as for pie dough. Press into bottom of a 9"x13" baking dish and bake 10 minutes at 350°. Meanwhile combine eggs, 1¼ c. brown sugar, pecans, coconut, 2 Tbl. flour, salt and vanilla. When 10 minutes is up pour pecan mixture into pan, spreading carefully so as not to dislodge pastry. Bake an additional 25–30 minutes or until puffed and set. While still warm make lemon glaze by combining powdered sugar with enough lemon juice to make a thin glaze. Spread it over the top of cookies. When cool cut in 1½ "x2" bars or diamonds.

Cheesecake Cookies

To make sixteen 2" x 2" cookies

Crust: ⅔ c. whole wheat flour
⅓ c. brown sugar
¼ c. sesame seeds
¼ c. chopped walnuts
⅓ c. butter, softened
Filling: 8 oz. cream cheese, softened
¼ c. honey
1 egg
2 tsp. lemon juice
1 tsp. vanilla

Combine crust ingredients and press into bottom of an 8" square baking pan. Bake at 350° for 10 minutes. While it is baking, beat cream cheese until soft and fluffy, then beat in remaining ingredients. Pour over crust and bake an additional 15–20 minutes of until filling is set. Let cool and refrigerate. Cookies may be topped with fresh fruit, strawberries, bananas, blackberries, etc. after baking.

Hazelnut Orange Cookies

To make three dozen cookies

4 oz. hazelnuts,
    toasted and finely chopped
½ c. butter, softened
2 c. + 1 Tbl. flour
⅔ c. sugar
2 egg yolks
1 tsp. vanilla
zest of 1 orange, juice of ½ orange

Mix all ingredients. Roll into a cylinder 1 ½" in diameter, wrap in plastic wrap and refrigerate till firm. Slice ¼ " thick. Place rounds on greased cookie sheet 1" apart and bake 10–15 minutes at 375°.

Shortbread

1 ½ c. unsalted butter
1 ¼ c. powdered sugar
1 ½ c. flour
1 ½ c. cornstarch
½ tsp. salt
1 tsp. vanilla

Cream butter and powdered sugar until light. Add flour and cornstarch gradually. Add salt and vanilla. If dough is sticky refrigerate an hour or so to firm. Otherwise press onto a baking sheet. Cover with waxed paper and use a rolling pin to roll the dough out to ⅝" thickness. Chill one hour. Remove waxed paper and prick dough thoroughly with tines of a fork. Bake at 325° 15–20 minutes or until just starting to color lightly. Taste a little bit of cookie; it should no longer taste of raw flour. Remove shortbread from oven and while still warm cut into squares or diamonds. May be dusted with powdered sugar when cool.

Note: Cornstarch makes shortbread meltingly delicate and tender. These cookies are very fragile. If you are making them to travel use 3 c. flour and eliminate the cornstarch. They'll still be good, just not as melt-in-your-mouth delicate.

Chocolate Truffle Cookies

To make three dozen small, or two dozen large cookies

2 oz. unsweetened chocolate

6 oz. semisweet chocolate

2 Tbl. butter

¼ c. flour

¼ tsp. baking powder

¼ tsp. salt

2 eggs

¾ c. sugar

2 tsp. instant coffee

1 tsp. vanilla

6 oz. chocolate chips

8 oz. chopped walnuts or pecans

Melt chocolates and butter over double boiler and set aside to cool. Sift together flour, baking powder and salt. Set aside. Beat eggs and sugar for a few minutes and add instant coffee and vanilla. Stir in melted chocolate, then flour, chocolate chips and nuts. Drop by spoonfuls (mixture will be very thick) onto greased cookie sheets. Bake 10-15 minutes at 350°.

Brownies

Another chocolate recipe where you have a lot of leeway in the baking process. A shorter baking period gives you the gooey chewy brownies that leave you licking your fingers, longer and you have the more respectable cake-type brownie.

To make twenty-four two inch brownies

4 oz. unsweetened baking chocolate
½ c. unsalted butter
4 eggs
1 ¾ c. sugar
1 tsp. vanilla
½ tsp. salt
1 c. flour
1 c. chopped nuts, optional

Melt the chocolate and butter in a double boiler and set aside to cool. Beat eggs with sugar, vanilla, and salt. Longer beating with an electric mixer will produce a lighter cake-like brownie, less beating a denser one. When the chocolate is cool stir into the egg mixture. Sift the flour into the bowl and fold in.

Add optional nuts. Pour batter into a greased 9"x13" baking pan and bake at 350° 20-30 minutes or until brownies are of desired consistency. Let cool (if possible) and cut in squares.

Cheesecake

To serve eight to twelve

12 oz. cream cheese, softened
2 eggs
½ c. sugar
1 tsp. vanilla
Topping: 1 c. sour cream
        ¼ c. sugar
        1 tsp. vanilla
Crust: 1 c. graham
        crackers crumbs
        2 Tbl. sugar
        2 oz. melted butter

Combine crust ingredients and press into bottom of a 9" spring-form pan. Blend cream cheese, eggs, sugar and vanilla till very smooth. Pour over crust. Bake 20 minutes at 375°. Combine topping ingredients, carefully spread over cheesecake and bake 5 minutes. Let cool, then chill before serving.

Chocolate Mousse Soufflé

This is one of the most versatile recipes I know. You can bake the mixture and eat it right away as a souffle, you can let it cool and eat it as a very dense flourless chocolate cake (I usually fill it with fruit and whipped cream), or you can bake half of it, let it cool and fill it with the other half as chocolate mousse. I guess the lesson is if it's chocolate it's edible.

To serve four to six

6 oz. semisweet
   or bittersweet chocolate
4 Tbl. unsalted butter
4 eggs, separated,
   plus two egg whites
pinch of salt
¼ c. sugar
1 tsp. vanilla
2–4 Tbl. Cointreau, cognac, rum
   or other liqueur, optional

Chop chocolate into small pieces and set in a double boiler to melt. When almost melted remove from heat and whisk to complete melting. Whisk in butter and then the egg yolks and the optional liqueur. Set aside. Start beating egg whites and the pinch of salt in a very clean bowl with a wire whisk or electric mixer. When soft peaks form beat in sugar. Beat until egg whites form stiff peaks. Stir ¼ of the egg whites into the chocolate mixture to lighten it, then fold in the remaining egg whites. Pour mixture into a souffle dish (or any fairly deep baking dish) that has been buttered and sprinkled with sugar. Souffle may wait up to an hour in a warm draft-free spot before baking. Fifteen minutes before you are ready to serve it place souffle in a 400° oven for 10 to 15 minutes. Although it's still good if cooked all the way through, my favorite way to eat this souffle is when it's set up as usual for a souffle around the outside but the center is still soft. That way when you serve it each person gets two desserts in one—a light puffy souffle and a bit of rich creamy hot mousse. I usually serve it with whipped cream; my sister insists vanilla ice cream is it.

Chocolate Mousse

Until recently I was never happy with my chocolate mousse—it always seemed too heavy and solid. I assumed the only way to make the mousse lighter was to use less chocolate, which I was loathe to do. Then one happy day I read a suggestion to slightly underbeat the egg whites and whipped cream. Because the chocolate is so substantial by itself they don't have to be beaten to the stiffness one usually does in order to support the mousse. My life is complete now; I can have all the chocolate and the gravity-defying lightness too.

To serve six to eight

12 oz. semisweet chocolate,
      chopped in small pieces
6 Tbl. milk or coffee
8 eggs, separated
pinch of salt
¼ tsp. cream of tartar
¼ c. sugar
1 c. heavy cream
Additional sweetened
      whipped cream for garnish

Melt chocolate with milk or coffee in a double boiler. When melted remove from heat and stir with a wire whisk till very smooth. One at a time beat in egg yolks. In a very clean bowl beat egg whites with salt and cream of tartar until very soft peaks form. Beat in sugar but stop beating before egg whites get stiff—they should just hold their shape when you lift the beaters, no more. In another bowl whip the cream, again only until soft peaks form. Quickly but gently stir ⅓ of the egg whites into the chocolate mixture to lighten it, then fold chocolate into the egg whites. Add the whipped cream and fold in until just mixed. Pour mousse into a pretty serving dish or into individual dishes—wine glasses are simple but attractive. Chill at least 3 hours. Serve garnished with whipped cream and shaved chocolate if desired.

Chocolate Truffles

This is the easiest candy to make because the chocolates don't have to be perfectly shaped; in fact they're supposed to look kind of lumpy and irregular, like a real truffle just dug up from under an oak tree. Tell everyone else that's what they are and maybe no one but you will eat them!

To make 2–3 dozen chocolates

1 lb. semisweet or bittersweet chocolate, the best you can find (*I use Callebaud, a Belgian chocolate; Lindt is also good*)

¾ c. heavy cream

1–2 Tbl. liqueur (optional) Grand Marnier, Kahlua, or Amaretto are possibilities

1–2 tsp. vegetable oil

½ c. unsweetened cocoa powder

Chop ½ lb. of the chocolate. Bring cream to a boil, remove from heat and add chocolate. Stir until chocolate is melted and mixture is smooth. Add liqueur. Refrigerate until firm but not hard—about 20-30 minutes. Put chocolate in a pastry bag with a large round tip about ¾" in. diameter. Pipe out rough shaped mounds of chocolate onto a sheet pan or plate.

Alternatively chocolates may be scooped out with a teaspoon. Commercially made truffles tend to be large, about 1 ½" in diameter; I prefer to make them smaller, about ¾–1". Chill pan 3–4 hours or overnight or until chocolates are very firm. Quickly and lightly roll chocolates between your palms to round them, but don't make them too perfect looking. Put chocolates back in the fridge while you melt the remaining chocolate for dipping.

Melt ½ lb. chocolate over a double boiler and let it cool to skin temperature. Stir in 1 tsp. oil; add more if needed to keep chocolate thin enough while you are dipping. Sift cocoa onto a plate. Drop chocolate mounds into melted chocolate and lift out with a fork, letting excess chocolate drip back into the pan. Gently place chocolate on the plate of cocoa. Continue dipping chocolates. After a few minutes chocolate coating will firm up and turn from shiny to dull; then you can roll the truffle around in the cocoa to coat it. Repeat until all truffles have been dipped and rolled in cocoa. If dipping chocolate gets too firm reheat gently over warm water, but don't let it get so warm it melts the chocolates when you drop them in.

Keep truffles refrigerated or frozen. (I usually label them as chicken livers or fish bait just to keep them around.) Let sit at room temperature 20 minutes (if refrigerated) to 1 hour (if frozen) before serving.

The Adobe and deck, 1938

Lemon Mousse

This recipe seems like a lot of work, requiring beating egg yolks, egg white meringue and cream. But it's worth it—perfectly light, creamy and lemony.

To serve six

6 egg yolks
⅔ c. sugar
juice of 3 lemons,
grated peel of 2 lemons
1 Tbl. gelatin,
    softened in 2 Tbl. cold water
1 ¼ c. heavy cream, whipped
Italian Meringue: 3 egg whites
                   ⅔ c. sugar
                   ⅓ c. water

Beat egg yolks, sugar, lemons and lemon peel over double boiler until hot and fluffy. Remove from heat, add gelatin and stir until dissolved. Continue beating (if possible put on mixer stand) till cool and very fluffy. Fold in whipped cream and Italian meringue. Pour into pretty serving bowl or individual parfait glasses. Chill 2 hours or more. Garnish with whipped cream and lemon peel.

To make meringue:
Place sugar and water in small heavy saucepan and bring to a boil. Cover and let simmer 5 minutes to wash down sugar crystals. Do not stir. Boil to soft ball stage. While sugar is cooking, beat egg whites until stiff peaks form. When sugar syrup is done pour over egg whites in a thin stream beating constantly. Continue beating till egg whites are cool and quite stiff.

Bread Pudding with Lemon Sauce

To serve eight

3 eggs

1 ¼ c. sugar

1 ½ tsp. vanilla

1 ¼ tsp. nutmeg

1 ¼ tsp. cinnamon

2 c. milk (or 1c. milk and 1 c. cream)

½ c. raisins

½ c. pecans, toasted and chopped

5 c. cubes of stale French bread
or a mixture of stale bread
and biscuits(*I save leftover sliced
bread, biscuits muffins, just about
anything except garlic bread, in the
freezer to use up this way*)

Lemon Sauce

sweetened whipped cream for
garnish

Beat the eggs a few minutes, preferably with an electric mixer, then add the sugar, vanilla, nutmeg and cinnamon and beat well. Beat in the milk, or milk and cream. Mix the raisins, pecans and bread cubes and place in a well buttered loaf pan. Pour the egg and milk mixture over them and let soak for 45 minutes, occasionally pushing down the bread cubes so they will completely absorb the milk. Push down any raisins on the surface— they will burn during baking. Preheat oven to 350° but lower it to 300° when pudding is placed in it. Bake 40 minutes, then increase temperature to 425° and bake another 15–20 minutes to puff and brown the pudding. Serve warm with lemon sauce and whipped cream.

Lemon Sauce

juice of 1 lemon

½ c. water

⅓ c. sugar

2 tsp. cornstarch

1 tsp. vanilla

Bring all ingredients except vanilla to a boil in a small saucepan. Boil one minute, stirring constantly. Remove from heat and stir in vanilla. Serve warm.

Buttercream Frosting

This is a very large amount of frosting; I can ice a small wedding cake with it. But it freezes well—how convenient to have an emergency batch of frosting at hand.

2 lb. butter
½ lb. shortening
5 lb. confectioners sugar
1 tsp. salt
2 Tbl. vanilla
½ lb. egg whites
1 Tbl. lemon juice

Beat butter and shortening till very light and fluffy. On low speed add sugar, salt and vanilla. Beat in egg whites and lemon juice. Beat till frosting is creamy and light. Enough frosting for 3–4 layer cakes. If frosting has been refrigerated let soften and beat well before using.

Butterscotch Sauce

To make one cup

⅓ c. light corn syrup
⅝ c. brown sugar
2 Tbl. butter
⅛ tsp. salt
⅓ c. cream
1 tsp. vanilla

Boil corn syrup, brown sugar, butter and salt to the consistency of heavy syrup, about 5 minutes. Let cool to luke warm and add cream and vanilla. Serve warm or cold on ice cream, cake or apple snow (Pg. 34). Sauce may be reheated in a double boiler.

Strawberry Shortcake

1 ¾ c. sifted flour

½ tsp. salt

1 Tbl. sugar

1 Tbl. baking powder

6 Tbl. unsalted butter

¾ c. milk

2–3 baskets
    perfectly ripe strawberries

¼ c. sugar

1 ½ c. whipping cream

¼ c. sugar

2 tsp. vanilla

Sift dry ingredients together. Cut in butter with a pastry blender until butter is incorporated and flour resembles coarse cornmeal. Add milk all at once and stir until dough forms a ball. Turn onto a floured surface and knead lightly 5 or 6 times. Roll out dough to ¾ in. thickness and cut in rounds with a biscuit cutter dipped in flour. Place on an ungreased baking sheet and bake at 450° 10–15 minutes or until puffed and golden brown.

Carefully wash and slice strawberries. Sprinkle with ¼ c. sugar and set aside to let sugar dissolve and make a syrup with the strawberries. Whip cream with ¼ c. sugar and vanilla until stiff.

To serve, split biscuits in half horizontally. Place bottom half of biscuit on dessert plate or bowl, cover with a spoonful of strawberries and one of whipped cream. Cover with top half of biscuit, more whipped cream and a generous spoonful of strawberries over all.

Washing strawberries and other fruits is quite a ritual in France. It is never done until the last minute—often bowls of water are placed on the dinner table so diners can dip their own. Strawberries should be placed gently in a bowl of cold water, then lifted out and laid on a towel to dry. No running water please. In fact, the best strawberries in France are specially grown with dust ruffles around each plant so they needn't be washed at all.

Mixed Berry Cobbler

To serve eight to ten

1 bag each, frozen, unsweetened:
   raspberries
   blueberries
   blackberries
½ c. sugar
3 Tbl. flour
Cobbler topping:
1 ½ c. flour
½ tsp. salt
¼ c. sugar
2 tsp. baking powder
6 Tbl. unsalted butter
¾ c. whipping cream

Mix together ½ c. sugar and 3 Tbl. flour and stir into berries. Place in a well-buttered 1 ½ qt. baking dish. Place baking dish, covered, in 375° oven to begin cooking while preparing topping. For the cobbler topping sift together the flour, salt, sugar, and baking powder. Cut in butter with pastry blender or two knives until mixture resembles coarse meal. Add cream and mix quickly. Remove berries from oven and dot the top of berries in dish with spoonfuls of the dough. Bake at 375° 15–20 minutes or until berries are bubbling, juices are clear and topping is puffed and brown. Serve warm with whipped cream or ice cream.

Berry Mousse

To serve six to eight

1 lb. package, frozen, unsweetened
 blackberries or raspberries
 or 1 pint fresh

scant ½ c. sugar or to taste

2 tsp. gelatin,
 softened in 3 Tbl. cold water

2 c., approx., heavy cream

Puree berries and force through a sieve to remove seeds. Measure. Sweeten to taste with sugar. Place softened gelatin over hot water until it is completely melted. Measure an amount of heavy cream equal to quantity of sieved berries and whip only until very soft peaks form—less than usual for whipped cream. Stir melted gelatin into berry puree very quickly and thoroughly—you don't want the gelatin to start congealing before it is completely incorporated into the puree. Then add the puree to the whipped cream and continue beating a few minutes until the mousse is just firm. Spoon into a pretty serving bowl or individual glasses—wine glasses do fine. Refrigerate one hour or more. Mousse may be garnished with whipped cream.

Apple Crisp

6 apples—Golden Delicious,
   Jonathan, or Granny Smith
   are good choices

½ c. raisins

½ c. walnuts

¼ c. honey

¼ c. frozen apple juice concentrate,
   thawed

½ c. butter, melted

½ c. flour, white or whole wheat
   or half and half

1 c. oats

1 tsp. cinnamon

1 tsp. vanilla

¾ c. brown sugar or honey

Vanilla ice cream
   or whipped cream

Peel, core and slice apples. Place in a buttered baking dish with the raisins and walnuts. Drizzle with honey and apple juice concentrate. Cover with buttered aluminum foil and bake at 350° 30 minutes. Meanwhile combine butter, flour, oats, cinnamon, vanilla and brown sugar or honey. Remove apples from oven and raise heat to 375°. Crumble topping over apples and return to oven for 20 minutes or until apples are tender and topping is brown. If topping browns too quickly, cover with aluminum foil. Serve crisp warm with vanilla ice cream or whipped cream.

Apple Snow

To serve six to eight

If you eliminate the butterscotch sauce this makes a low calorie, fat-free, dairy - free dessert.

4 egg whites
½ tsp. cream of tartar
3 c. cold, thick apple sauce
  (if using store-bought I cook it another 15 minutes to make it nice and thick, and I use 1c. apple butter in place of one of the cups of apple sauce)
½–¾ c. butterscotch sauce (pg. 184)

Beat the egg whites until foamy; add the cream of tartar. Beat at high speed until egg whites form stiff shiny peaks. On low speed add apple sauce by the ½ cupful. Beat 1 minute at high speed or until mixture holds its shape softly in a spoon. Refrigerate up to 2 hours before serving (one hour or less is best). Spoon apple snow into goblets or parfait glasses and drizzle butterscotch sauce over all.

Apricot Sorbet

To serve six

2 cans whole apricots
2 egg whites
½ c. sugar
2 Tbl. lemon juice
2–3 drops almond extract

Drain apricots, saving juice. Puree in blender or food processor and add enough juice to make 2 cups. Beat egg whites till they form soft peaks. Add sugar, lemon juice and almond extract to apricots. Fold in beaten egg whites. Pour into shallow bowl and freeze. When almost solid beat vigorously to break up crystals then refreeze. Beat and refreeze once more. Serve with sweetened whipped cream if desired and sliced apricots or raspberries.

Fruit Sorbet

For a 4 qt. ice cream freezer, enough for 12-16 servings

Since freezing reduces the intensity of flavor somewhat be sure and use fruit at the peak of their season when they are sweetest and most flavorful.

3 qt. pureed fresh fruit
(I prefer one fruit sorbets,
 but some combinations are great, strawberry-banana for example)

cantaloupe	honeydew	pineapple
watermelon	strawberries	blueberries
blackberries	bananas	

(if combining banana with another flavor add it carefully; it tends to overpower other flavors)

¼–½ c. sugar to bring out the flavor of the fruit. (*This is far less than most recipes, but I just don't see why sorbets have to be so sweet. Commercially it makes sense because it prolongs shelf life, but homemade sorbets and ice creams don't deserve that kind of treatment. They want to be made and devoured. Also, with so little sugar it will dissolve easily in the fruit and you don't have to make a sugar syrup. With pineapple sorbet I sweeten the puree with frozen pineapple juice concentrate instead of sugar, one 12 oz. can of concentrate pineapple per pineapple.*)

Place puree in ice cream freezer and freeze as directed.

Fruit Curry

Selection of fresh fruit, at least 3 kind, cut in chunks:

pineapple	peaches	apples
mango	bananas	cherries
papaya	pears	strawberries

Sauce:

8 Tbl. butter
¼ c. sugar
¼ c. brown sugar
¼ c. lemon juice
1 tsp. cinnamon
2 tsp. ginger
grating of fresh nutmeg
½ c. dark rum

Melt butter in saucepan. Add remaining ingredients and simmer 5 minutes.

Condiments:

grated chocolate
chopped toasted almonds
raisins or currants
chopped candied ginger
chopped mint
coconut

Serve platter of fruit at table with bowls of sauce and condiments.

To eat: dip chunks of fruit in sauce, then in condiment.

Fruit Soufflé

To serve six

1 pint strawberries (or raspberries,
    black berries or blueberries)
    hulled, and pureed
1 tsp. lemon juice
1 tsp. orange liqueur
⅓ c. sugar
5 eggs, separated
¼ tsp. cream of tartar
2 quart soufflé mold,
    buttered generously
    and sprinkled with sugar

Heat fruit, lemon juice, liqueur and sugar. Bring to a simmer and stir until sugar is dissolved. Remove from heat and pour over egg yolks, stirring constantly. Beat egg whites with cream of tartar in a very clean bowl until stiff. Fold in hot fruit puree and pour into soufflé mold. Bake at 375° 15–20 minutes or until puffed and just set in center. Serve immediately.

Pumpkin Ice Cream Dessert

To serve eight to ten

½ gal. vanilla ice cream
3 tsp. cinnamon
½ tsp. ea. cloves, nutmeg,
(mace, all spice; optional)
1 lg. can pumpkin puree
1 box ginger snaps
1 c. sweetened whipped cream
pecan halves for garnish

Soften ice cream. Add spices and pumpkin. Add more seasonings if needed to bring out pumpkin pie flavor. Place ginger snaps in one layer in a 9"x13" baking dish. Cover with ½ ice cream mixture. Add another layer of cookies and the rest of the ice cream. Cover with plastic wrap and refreeze at least 2 hours before serving. If dessert has become very hard remove from freezer 20 minutes , cut in 3"x4" squares, garnish with whipped cream and a pecan half.

Index of Recipes

Almond
    Almond Paté 61
    Banana Pie 155
    Chocolate Cake with Scotch ..169
    Curried Tuna Salad 95
    Fennel Chicken 105
    Pear and Almond Tart 158
Andy's Banana Bread 23
Apple
    Apple Carrot Muffins 19
    Apple Cider Dressing 84
    Apple Crisp 188
    Apple Snow 189
    Curried Tuna Salad 95
    Sour Cream Apple Pie 156
    Tarte Tatin 157
Appetizers 49–61
Apricot Sorbet 189
Avocado
    Avocado Dressing 85
    Guacamole 52
    Layered Bean Dip 52
    Red Barn Dressing 86
Bacon
    Potato, Bacon
    and Cheese Soup 38
    Scallops in Bacon
    and Cognac Sauce 122
    Spaghetti alla Carbonara 68
Bagna Cauda 56
Baked Fish
    with Mushroom Sauce 116
Baked Polenta 74
Baked Pumpkin Soup 45
Banana
    Andy's Banana Bread 23
    Banana Bran Muffins 20
    Banana Bread II 23
    Banana Pie 155

Barbeque Sauce 100
Basil
    Lasagna 67
    Pasta Oopla 66
    Pesto Sauce 65
    Tomato Pesto Canapés 60
    Tomato Pesto Tart 131
Beans and Legumes
    Hummus 137
    Layered Bean Dip 52
    Turkey Chili 111
    Vegetarian Chili 142
Berry Mousse 187
Beurre Blanc 120
Beurre Nantais 120
Biscuit Sandwiches 56
Biscuits, Whole Wheat 18
Black Bottom Pie 153
Blueberry
    Blueberry Muffins 20
    Mixed Berry Cobbler 186
Borscht 47
Bran Muffins 19
Bread Pudding 183
Breads
    Andy's Banana Bread 23
    Banana Bread II 23
    Bread, basic 14
    Challah 17
    Church Cornbread 21
    Cornbread 21
    Irish Soda Bread 24
    Jalapeño Cornbread 22
    Spoonbread 22
Brownies 177
Buttercream Frosting 184
Buttermilk
    Banana Bread II 23
    Borscht 47

Bran Muffins 19
Buttermilk Coffeecake 24
Buttermilk Rosemary Oven
Fried Chicken 110
Chocolate Buttermilk Cake 167
Irish Soda Bread 24
Rocky Road Cake 171
Whole Wheat Biscuits 18
Butterscotch Sauce 184
Cabbage Salad, Red 94
Cakes 159–172
Caponata 57
Caribbean Chicken 100
Carrot
    Apple Carrot Muffins 19
    Carrot Cake I 159
    Carrot Cake II 159
    Carrot Ginger Soup 35
Cashews
    Banana Pie 155
    Curried Rice Salad with
    Cashews and Raisins 93
    Hoisin Chicken
    with Cashews 109
    Vegetarian Loaf 140
Challah 17
Cheese
    Cheesecake 177
    Cheesecake cookies 174
    Cream Cheese Frosting 160
    Cream Cheese Pastry 149
    Garden Dip 87
    Gorgonzola Pasta 70
    Greek Shrimp in Tomato and
    Feta Cheese Sauce 123
    Hot Potato Salad
    with Sausage 91
    Jalapeño Cornbread 22
    Lasagna 67

Makis 54
Mom's Squash Casserole 132
Mushroom Piroshki 58
Mystery Pecan Pie..................152
Omelette Soufflé Roll..............26
Onion Soup 37
Pasta alla Putanesca 69
Pesto Sauce.............................65
Potato, Bacon
and Cheese Soup 38
Potatoes au Gratin with Ham 134
Red Cabbage Salad 94
Roquefort Butter.......................59
Roquefort Radish Canapés 59
Snow Peas Stuffed
with Smoked Salmon...............53
Spaghetti alla Carbonara.........68
Spanokopita 143
Tomato Pesto Tart 131
Vegetarian Loaf 140
Chicken
Chicken Liver Mousse 55
Chicken Entrees 99–111
Chinese Chicken Salad 96
Ginger Pineapple Chicken 54
Spicy Peanut Sauce
for Noodles 75
Chocolate
Black Bottom Pie 153
Brownies.................................177
Chocolate Cakes 166–172
Chocolate Frosting 166
Chocolate Glaze......................169
Chocolate Mousse 179
Chocolate Mousse Cake 165
Chocolate Mousse Soufflé.....178
Chocolate Truffle Cookies 176
Chocolate Truffles...................180
Church Cornbread 21
Cilantro
Mexican Grilled Chicken with
Lime Marinade 101
Salmon Seviche.......................53
Salsa...51
Spicy Thai Marinade
for Fish 115

Turkey Chili 111
Cookies 173–177
Cookie-Type Pastry Dough 149
Corn
Baked Polenta 74
Church Cornbread 21
Cornbread 21
Jalapeño Cornbread 22
Spoonbread 22
Cream Cheese Frosting 160
Cream Cheese Pastry 149
Cream of Mushroom Soup 40
Curry
Curried Rice Salad with
Raisins and Cashews 93
Curried Squash and
Mushroom Soup 41
Curried Tuna Salad..................95
Curried Zucchini Soup............44
Curry Mayonnaise 95
Fruit Curry 191
Spinach and Tofu Curry.........137
Dips for Vegetables
Bagna Cauda 56
Caponata 57
Gado Gado 136
Guacamole 52
Desserts.............................145–192
Easy Chocolate Cake 172
Eggplant
Caponata 57
Ratatouille 130
Ratatouille Soup 46
Fennel Chicken 105
Fish and Seafood
Curried Tuna Salad..................95
Fish and Seafood
Entrees 113–126
Salmon Seviche 53
Snow Peas Stuffed
with Smoked Salmon...............53
French Dressing........................83
Fresh Ginger Gingerbread 160
Frostings
Buttercream 184
Chocolate 166

Chocolate Glaze........................169
Cream Cheese Frosting 160
Pecan Frosting 163
Rocky Road Frosting 171
Fruit Curry 191
Fruit Sorbet..............................190
Fruit Soufflé 192
Gado Gado 136
Garden Dip...............................87
Gaspacho 43
Genoise (Sponge Cake) 164
Ginger
Carrot Ginger Soup..................35
Chicken Teriyaki Marinade ...101
Fresh Ginger Gingerbread 160
Lemon Ginger Chicken 107
Spicy Thai Marinade
for Fish 115
Gorgonzola Pasta 70
Granola 25
Greek Shrimp in Tomato and Feta
Cheese Sauce 123
Guacamole 52
Harriet's Pecan Pie......................151
Hazelnut Orange Cookies............175
Herman's Lemon Chicken 106
Hoisin Chicken
with Cashews..........................109
Hollandaise Sauce......................121
Honey
Honey Mustard Dressing..........83
Honey Orange Syrup...............25
Lemon Parsley
Honey Dressing.......................87
Hors D'oeuvres........................49–61
Hot Potato Salad with Sausage 91
Hummus..................................137
Irish Soda Bread 24
Jalapeño Cornbread 22
Jícama Orange Salad 97
Lasagna....................................67
Layered Bean Dip.......................52
Lemon
Bread Pudding with Lemon
Sauce 183
Herman's Lemon Chicken 106

Lemon Ginger Chicken 107
Lemon Mousse 182
Lemon Parsley Honey
Dressing................................87
Lemon Pasta............................73
Lemon Tart.............................150
Lemon Teriyaki Shark 118
Soy Garlic Lemon Butter........129
Lime
Mexican Grilled Chicken with
Lime Marinade.....................101
Salmon Seviche........................53
Spicy Thai Marinade
for Fish...............................115
Linguini with
White Clam Sauce....................71
Lobster Pasta............................72
Makis.......................................54
Marinade for Tofu..................139
Marinara Sauce........................64
Mayonnaise..............................88
Mexican Grilled Chicken with
Lime Marinade.....................101
Minestrone Soup......................42
Mixed Berry Cobbler...............186
Mom's Squash Casserole..........132
Mousse
Berry Mousse.........................187
Chicken Liver Mousse.............55
Chocolate Mousse..................179
Chocolate Mousse Soufflé......178
Lemon Mousse.......................182
Muffins...............................19–20
Mushrooms
Baked Fish with
Mushroom Sauce..................116
Chicken Cacciatore.................102
Cream of Mushroom Soup......40
Curried Squash and
Mushroom Soup.....................41
Mushroom Piroshki..................58
Portuguese Baked Fish...........117
Seafood in Cream Sauce.........125
Stuffed Filet of Sole................119
Mustard
Honey Mustard Dressing.........83

Mustard Dill Dressing..............80
Poulet au Diable....................103
Tarragon Mustard Dressing....82
Mystery Pecan Pie..................152
Nut Tart with Chocolate Glaze..154
Oatmeal Cookies 173
Omelette Soufflé Roll...............26
Onion Soup 37
Orange
Hazelnut Orange Cookies......175
Jícama Orange Salad................97
Orange Vinaigrette...................81
Orange Yogurt Dressing..........81
Sesame Orange Dressing.........82
Wild Rice Salad with
Oranges and Pecans................93
Oyster Stew, My Dad's..............126
Pasta 63–75
Pastry 147–158
Biscuit Sandwiches..................56
Mixed Berry Cobbler..............186
Mushroom Piroshki..................58
Strawberry Shortcake.............185
Tomato Pesto Tart...................131
Whole Wheat Biscuits..............18
Paté, Almond...........................61
Pea
Pea and Spinach Soup..............39
Split Pea Soup..........................44
Peanut
Banana Pie.............................155
Gado Gado..............................136
Spicy Peanut Sauce
for Noodles............................75
Pear and Almond Tart..............158
Pecans
Banana Pie.............................155
Bread Pudding........................183
Carrot Cake.............................159
Chocolate Truffle Cookies.....176
Easy Chocolate Cake..............172
Harriet's Pecan Pie.................151
Mystery Pecan Pie..................152
Nut Tart with
Chocolate Glaze....................154
Pecan Bars.............................174

Pecan Frosting 163
Pecan Fudge Pie 154
Spiced Pecan Cake 163
Sweet Potatoes with Tangerines
and Pecans............................135
Wild Rice Salad with Oranges
and Pecans..............................93
Peppers, Sweet Red
Ratatouille 130
Ratatouille Soup 46
Stuffed Peppers
Genovese Style.......................133
Pesto
Pesto Sauce...............................65
Tomato Pesto Tart..................131
Photo Galerie Chocolate Cake....170
Polenta, Baked.........................74
Poppy Seed Dressing................84
Portuguese Baked Fish.............117
Potato
Hot Potato Salad
with Sausage...........................91
Potato Bacon and
Cheese Soup...........................38
Potato Salad.............................90
Potatoes au Gratin
with ham...............................134
Red Chard and Potato Soup....36
Poulet au Diable
(Deviled Chicken)...................103
Pumpkin
Baked Pumpkin Soup..............45
Pumpkin Ice Cream
Dessert.................................192
Ratatouille..............................130
Ratatouille Soup.......................46
Red Barn Dressing....................86
Red Cabbage Salad....................94
Red Chard and Potato Soup.......36
Rice
Curried Rice Salad...................93
Rice Salad.................................92
Stuffed Peppers
Genovese Style.......................133
Tahini Tamari Topping
for Rice and Vegetables.........138

Vegetarian Loaf 140
Wild Rice Salad 93
Roast Chicken with
    Forty Cloves of Garlic.............104
Rocky Road Cake 171
Rocky Road Frosting 171
Roquefort Butter..............................59
Roquefort Radish Canapés 59
Saffron Mayonnaise 46
Salads 90–97
Salad Dressings 80–89
Salmon Ceviche 53
Salsa Cocida 51
Salsa Cruda 51
Salsa or Gaspacho Dressing.........85
Salsa Verde.......................................51
Sauces
    Barbeque Sauce.....................100
    Beurre Blanc............................120
    Beurre Nantais........................120
    Butterscotch Sauce 184
    Cream Sauce 124
    Hollandaise Sauce 121
    Lemon Sauce (sweet) 183
    Tahini Tamari Topping 138
    White Sauce..............................124
Seafood
    Entrees 113–126
    Linguini with
    White Clam Sauce 71
    Lobster Pasta............................72
    Shrimp Salad with Grapes.......97
Sesame Orange Dressing 82
Shortbread.....................................175
Shrimp Salad with Grapes............97
Snow Peas Stuffed
    with Smoked Salmon................53
Soups..29–47
Sorbet
    Apricot 189
    Fruit...190
Soufflés
    Chocolate Mousse Soufflé......178
    Fruit Soufflé 192
    Omelette Soufflé Roll................26
Sour Cream Apple Pie.................156

Soy Garlic Lemon Butter.............129
Spaghetti alla Carbonara..............68
Spanokopita 143
Spiced Pecan Cake 162
Spicy Peanut Sauce
    for Noodles 75
Spicy Thai Marinade
    for Fish 115
Spinach
    Pea and Spinach Soup 39
    Spanokopita 143
    Spinach and Tofu Curry........137
Split Pea Soup 44
Sponge Cake 164
Spoonbread 22
Squash
    Curried Squash and
    Mushroom Soup.......................41
    Curried Zucchini Soup.............44
    Minestrone Soup 42
    My Mom's
    Squash Casserole 132
    Ratatouille 130
    Ratatouille Soup 46
Strawberry Rhubarb Pie..............157
Strawberry Shortcake 185
Stuffed Filet of Sole.....................119
Stuffed Peppers
    Genovese Style........................133
Sweet Potatoes with
    Tangerines and Pecans 135
Tabouleh salad................................94
Tahini Tamari Topping 138
Tarragon Mustard Dressing 82
Tarte Tatin 157
Tofu
    Marinade for Tofu 139
    Spinach Tofu Curry 137
Tomato
    Chicken Cacciatore 102
    Gaspacho 43
    Greek Shrimp in Tomato and
    Feta Cheese Sauce 123
    Marinara Sauce 64
    Minestrone Soup 42
    Pasta alla Putanesca.................69

Ratatouille 130
Ratatouille Soup...........................46
Salsa Cocida 51
Salsa Cruda 51
Salsa or Gaspacho Dressing.....85
Tomato Pesto Canapés 60
Tomato Pesto Tart 131
Tomato Sandwich 141
Turkey Chili 111
Vegetarian Chili.........................142
Turkey Chili 111
Vegetable Soup, Basic...................34
Vegetables, Flavor-Preserving
    Ways to Cook...........................128
Vegetarian Chili.............................142
Vegetarian Loaf 140
Vinaigrette, Basic............................80
Walnuts
    Banana Bread 23
    Brownies...................................177
    Buttermilk Coffeecake 24
    Carrot Cake 159
    Chocolate Truffle Cookies 176
    Easy Chocolate Cake 172
    Gorgonzola Pasta 70
    Nut Tart with
    Chocolate Glaze......................154
    Oatmeal Cookies 173
    Pesto Sauce 65
    Red Cabbage Salad 94
    Rocky Road Frosting 171
    Roquefort Butter........................59
    Vegetarian Loaf 140
White Sauce....................................124
Whole Wheat Biscuits...................18
Wild Rice with
    Oranges and Pecans.................93
Wine Cake 161
Zucchini
    Curried Zucchini Soup............44
    My Mom's
    Squash Casserole....................132
    Ratatouille 130
    Ratatouille Soup 46

To order more copies of this book,
send the order form below to:

Westerbeke Ranch Conference Center
2300 Grove St.
Sonoma, CA 95476

Or to order by phone with your credit card,
Call (707) 996-7546

	Quantity	Cost	Total
A Plate of Grace Cookbook		@ $14.95 ea	
Tax (Calif. residents add 7.5%)			
Postage $2.50 per item			
AMOUNT ENCLOSED			

Card # _____ exp date _____

Please send above items to:

(name) _____

(address) _____

_____

GIFT ORDERS

Please send _____ copies of the COOKBOOK
to:

_____

_____

_____

*(For additional gifts, please enclose
name/address & gift card option on a
separate sheet of paper).*

☐ Enclose a gift card from:

(name(s) as it should appear on card)

_____

_____